You've Got the Power!

Four Paths to Awaken Your Body's Archetypal Energies

LAVINIA PLONKA

MAVEN PRESS, ASHEVILLE, NC

© 2022 Lavinia Plonka
ISBN: 978-1-66786-152-4
All Rights Reserved

Original Illustrations by Ron Morecraft
Additional Graphics by Sarah Vick

www.laviniaplonka.com

Other Books by Lavinia Plonka

What Are You Afraid Of:
A Body/Mind Guide to Courageous Living

Walking Your Talk: Changing Your Life Through The Magic of Body Language

The Little Book of Falling (and Getting Up)

Know Thyself – The Oracle at Delphi

Table of Contents

Introduction

The Beginning

"I don't know why we bother with you, you are absolutely useless. You're going to end up being nothing but a bum when you grow up." This was the repeated tirade I endured, along with beatings and other punishments, till I escaped my home at age eighteen.

I know that many people have had worse childhoods than mine. But my own was bad enough. Plenty of books and memoirs have detailed for readers the terror of an alcoholic household, of being punished "for your own good," and the endless struggle against chaos. There are still entire years of my childhood that I can't remember, probably for the best. My siblings' and my coping mechanism was comedy, turning the downstairs' scenes of madness into upstairs' entertainments for ourselves, creating silly characters and puppet shows that turned the beatings into slapstick and the nightmares into clown scenarios. We all went into comedy in some fashion as a profession. I became a clown and mime: a romantic if not exactly lucrative profession.

I spent my young adult life sabotaging everything I touched in order to not make my dad a liar. When I did succeed at something, he mocked me for my choices: of husband, of career, of lifestyle. When as a mature adult I realized that nothing I did would ever please my parents, there was still a little girl who would surface, wanting someone, just once, to tell me I was a "good girl."

Life became a search: for meaning, for happiness, for pain relief, for understanding. It took many years and many disastrous detours on my personal hero's journey to learn that all of these searches are connected. The deeper I went into my healing process, the more I learned about the patterns I carried in my thinking, feeling, posture, movement . . . As I unpacked my emotional baggage, I began to uncover the sources of my suffering and my failures, which were contained within my physical habits. This book is the distillation of years of research, searching, and self-study. If you are reading this book, you share this curiosity and desire for "realizing your dreams." I believe that by tuning into your relationship with your body, you can literally become the change you want to see in the world.

Emotions, Mythology, and the Body

As a dancer and mime artist, I was always drawn to the expression of emotions. While I was adept at portraying sadness, joy, lust, and rage, I had no understanding of why we take on these postures and attitudes. Why did certain people attract me? Why did I shrink in the face of certain situations? My search led me to study many traditions: Yoga, tarot, Buddhism, G.I Gurdjieff. I was even in a Seth Speaks group, where we listened to a reel-to-reel recording of an entity channeled through a woman named Jane Roberts somewhere in upstate New York. But it wasn't until I discovered the writings of Dr. Moshe Feldenkrais that I began to understand how I was carrying my history in the way I walked, talked, loved, and fought. This sent me off on another journey of researching the relationship between movement and neuroscience, chemistry, anatomy and mythology, yes, mythology.

Each culture's myths tell the story of human behavior: the capricious Greek gods, the heroic sagas of the Norse and Celtic heroes, the talented Yoruban Orishas. The characters in myths represent archetypal personalities that reflect a culture's world view. I'll never forget the shock I experienced when I learned, when well into my fifties, that Shakespeare's Hamlet was not an original story, but derived from an ancient Finnish tale about Amletus, which turned out to be a myth explaining the precession of the equinoxes.

Mythological characters have long been the subject of psychological and archetypal study. The word "archetype" comes from two Greek words that can be translated together to mean the "beginning type," or as some people have interpreted, an essence. The Greek philosopher Plato believed certain ideas or qualities are imprinted on the human soul. Karl Jung named twelve basic archetypes, from hero to lover. Author Carolyn Myss lists over a hundred possibilities in her books on archetypes. You can see the influence of myth in some of the labels that have become part of popular culture: the Peter Pan syndrome, narcissism (named after the youth Narcissus who fell in love with his reflection), making a Herculean effort, etc. At any given moment, you could choose to identify with a particular archetype, and the mind boggles at the myriad possibilities for analysis and self-study around the cast of characters that lives inside each of us. Every encounter with another person, every decision point, every life challenge can call forth the behavior of one of Jung's or Myss's archetypes. This is a wonderful study, and there are plenty of books and courses that explore this.

The Power of Four

Four archetypes continually appear in culture and mythology: the Warrior, Teacher, Healer, and Visionary. The number four lives in literature and language: The Four Pillars of Destiny, the four corners of the earth, the four directions or winds, the four seasons, the four dignities. You can find representatives of these four archetypes everywhere; for example: The warrior knights of the Round Table in England; the legendary teacher Lao-Tzu from China; Sonzwaphi, the Bushman Healing deity; and Kumugwe, the visionary god of the Pacific Northwest. These four iconic energies inhabit and inspire the human psyche. You meet them now in Beyonce's fierce yet beautiful music videos personifying her warrior side, or in the visionary

3

creations of Steve Jobs. We are constantly being touched and influenced by the archetypes' appearance in the world.

I first encountered these four archetypes in the writing of the late anthropologist Angeles Arrien, who presented them from the perspective of Native American wisdom traditions. I dove deeper, exploring the gifts and challenges of these four archetypes within myself. Connections emerged: between parts of the body, certain ways we move, and human qualities. At some point I realized that my attraction to these archetypes was not just curiosity-based. It also stemmed from the fact that to me, they represented potential. Like the four pillars of my own destiny, I saw them as supporting me to become the change I wanted to see in the world.

There is something irresistible in exploring typology. Meyers-Briggs developed an entire industry around it. Certain archetype studies emphasize the need to label, offering quizzes to find out your business archetype or your romantic archetype. Whether it's Human Design or the Enneagram, we love to know what "type" we are. I'm old enough to remember a popular pick-up line from the '70s, "Hi there, my name's John. So what's your sign?" Sometimes it even worked!

Labels can also limit you. When you call yourself a "seven" or a "projector" or a "Scorpio," it can close off other avenues. Enneagram teacher Russ Hudson has said that instead of putting yourself in a box with a number, you should "choose the number that will help you grow the most." This book invites you to explore how each of these four archetypes lives within you as opposed to looking for your "type." You are not simply a "teacher type" or a "visionary." By experiencing the gifts and challenges of each one, you will learn to choose appropriate actions and behaviors to support you on your journey.

How to Use This Book

The book is broken into several parts. In Part I, you will first meet the archetypes from the perspective of essential qualities that are reflected in a part of the anatomy: a center of presence. You will also meet some of the "shadows" of each archetype. Part II introduces what I call the kryptonite of each archetype. For those of you not familiar with Superman comics, kryptonite is the Achilles' heel of the famous American superhero Superman, the only substance that can destroy his power. No one on this planet is free of their personal kryptonite, but often, we don't recognize it until it has drained us. Part III dives into what I call their superpowers. Like the superheroes in our comic books, the archetypes have qualities that are representative of their highest possibilities. You don't have to know how to fly in order to be your best self. But you can develop heightened awareness and resources that make what right now seems impossible, possible, and even fun. As you explore the center of presence, the superpower, and the kryptonite of each archetype, you will be able to harness and utilize the boundless resources within yourself.

I have chosen to present the archetypes in a specific order, but I really could have started with any of them. Instead of looking at this as a linear process, think of the book as a web or a tapestry of ideas. You'll see how these, as Plato put it, "essences" interact with and support each other. In the process, you will acquire what you need to manifest your own possibilities.

Sometimes, based on culture, education, and conditioning, people find themselves predisposed to resonate or reject a certain archetype. "I don't like conflict; I just don't like the idea of having a warrior in me." "How can the healer be part of me when I can't heal?" "I've always been a teacher, I love teaching, I want to know more about why!" "Yeah, I've always had great ideas, great plans, but they never materialize. What good is it to be a visionary if none of my visions come about?" These are all statements I've heard in my classes and are beautiful examples of aspects of a person's self-image. I am this, not that. Another label.

Instead, allow your curiosity to guide you. Feel free to start with the one you like. But don't avoid the one you dislike! There may be very good reasons for your aversion.

About Movement

"Movement is life. Life is a process. Improve the process and you improve life itself." – Moshe Feldenkrais

As mentioned earlier, you carry your story in your posture and gestures, your breath, and even your voice. Your walk is so unique, an old friend would recognize you from a block away from behind! You are the result of a lifetime of learning and choices that have become habit, wired in every step you take. That is why, in order to understand your archetypal choices, you want to not just absorb the information intellectually but embody it. The most direct way to realize this is through movement.

The media is full of stories and statistics about the importance of movement. Researchers are calling sitting the new smoking. "Walking daily helps you think better" is an oft-repeated statement. Fitness apps are everywhere. However, many forms of exercise omit a connection between the mind, body, and emotions as if the body is simply like a car that needs to run while the driver is busy doing something else: listening to podcasts while out walking, watching videos while on the treadmill. The embodiment exercises in this book invite you to bring your parts together, so that thinking, feeling, and sensation are all on the same page.

It may be tempting to skip the movement exercises or just read them without trying them. But I encourage you to play with them; they will enrich your experience of what you are reading. Most of the explorations have been written in a manner that allow you to experiment as you are reading, or perhaps by putting the book down for a moment to explore. However, if you wish to go deeper, I have included a QR code in certain chapters that link you to a page that contains relevant audio lessons that you can access at your convenience. Or visit https://laviniaplonka.com/archetype-move-ment-lessons/ for the lessons. They are intended to deepen your experience.

PART I

Meet the Archetypes

CHAPTER 1

Your History, Your Biology, Your Journey

You begin to learn even before you are born, listening to the sounds of voices while in the womb.[i] After birth, you begin to develop your self-image and your relationship with the outside world. Genetics plays a part in who you are: the color of your eyes, your bone structure, etc. These will develop according to your DNA. (I can try all I want and can't seem to get taller than 5'2"!) Some will say you are born with a soul or essence that informs your personhood. But regardless of destiny, karma, sacred contracts, or soul retrieval, how you process the information flooding in through your senses, how you receive impressions from the world outside, as well as how you experience your inner life create the process that unfolds as uniquely "you."

We are fed by food and air, but we evolve as a result of how we receive and digest the massive amount of information being offered at every second. We call this learning, which through repetition becomes habit. For example, you may have a skeletal habit of always wanting to orient to the right. Did that start in infancy, when the window in your room was on the right side of your crib? Or was the window on the left, and the light hurt your eyes, so you learned to turn away, developing the rightward habit? Either way, the story remains in your skeleton, your movement choices, even how you orient in the world. Multiply that small thing with the millions of pieces of information that you receive every day. Your brain receives and processes the sunlight outside your window, the sound of your mother singing, the siren that startled you out of a nap . . . everything. What impressions fed you as you grew up? And what ate away at you, reducing your vitality? Sometimes the story is the result of repetition; words you repeatedly heard or actions you repeated over and over till they became a part of you. Sometimes the story stems from a big event; we even literally say, "It left an impression on me."

You are constantly absorbing stories: from the media, your interactions with others, and the stories you tell yourself. These stories help you make sense of your feelings in order to make life choices. What you call emotions are neurochemical responses that create sensations inside you. These sensations cause you to breathe, move, and respond to life situations in a particular way. You give these sensations names: sadness, anger, jealousy, giddiness. Or maybe the name eludes you, and it's just good/bad. That is your story. This can lead to telling a story about the story: I'm sad because I never get what I ask for. I'm angry because he doesn't respect me.

These basic principles then evolve into behavioral choices, reflected in myths and fairy tales; eternal themes that inspire great stories like Star Wars or Black Panther, and archetypal characters like Yoda and Wonder Woman. Emotions impact how you stand, move, and manifest in the world. We speak of a heroic stance, a compassionate gaze, a shady demeanor. The neurochemical relationship between your interior state and how you walk, talk, and act is the embodiment of your lifetime of acquired habits. There is even new evidence that how you breathe as a child affects the shape of your face.[ii] Abraham Lincoln has been quoted (perhaps apocryphally) to say, "You can't do anything about the face you were born with, but your face at fifty is all your fault." You can't simultaneously untangle what's happening in your face with your breathing patterns, your posture, your walk, and your life's history. It took years to create all your patterns and habits. For that reason,

I've zeroed in on four parts of our anatomy that offer a focus for each of the four archetypes. Since every part of you is connected to every other part, you will see how these four "centers of presence" interact with each other, just as your archetypal choices blend to create your unique way of being in the world. Throughout this book, you will encounter "going deeper" questions that examine how these impressions have influenced your life's trajectory.

Your Body IS Your Mind

There are many ways to learn about how different archetypes influence your life choices. One powerful way is, as the Sufis say, "as close as your jugular vein," so obvious as to be invisible. It is your own body—how you stand, walk, talk, and breathe. Every second, your entire organism is making choices for how to manifest in this world. As mentioned earlier, your way of being is uniquely yours, based on your education, conditioning, and of course, your genetics.

How do you stand? Walk? Where are your tensions? What is your posture like? You might say, "Well, this is just how I am." But many of these qualities were once choices and are now habits. These habits influence your relationship to the four archetypes we will explore. Before you dive into the possibilities presented in this book, let's look at where you are right now. What is your self-image now?

I'm often reminded of this Zen *koan*: "When you're not thinking of anything good and anything bad, at that moment, what is your original face?" While there are many levels to contemplating this, you know that every moment, you are carrying your face, with all its reactions, impressions, and history with you. The face is inextricably linked to posture, thinking, and emotions. A lifetime of contemplation might not get you to your "original" face, but you can begin to see and sense how and who you are right now.

Can you sense your face right now—from the inside? Which direction do your lips go? Turned up, down? Many people have one up and one down. Notice your jaw; are your teeth together? If so, do your teeth line up? Is your chin forward or down? What do you sense in your forehead? How do your eyes feel?

You can see how this process of self-examination could be endless. The massive amount of detail in every human's physical organization is a treasure trove. You can begin to simply observe, like an anthropologist, the map of yourself. Two arms, two legs, a head, and a trunk. There are esoteric traditions that use the image of the five-pointed star to illustrate both the human body and our relationship with the cosmic order. You can learn to see this map or star shape in yourself.

As you explore the following embodiment exercise, keep in mind that there is no wrong way to do this. The important factor is how you pay attention, not how you follow instructions, or if you are doing what you think you *should* be doing. Think of this as an introduction to a new way of seeing yourself and just enjoy the process. You can simply click on the QR Code for an audio version of the following so you can follow along with your eyes closed, a wonderful way to go "inside."

What Is Your Shape?

- Stand or lie down with your legs elongated.

- Close your eyes. Picture a line that extends from your belly down your right leg. Sense its length. Maybe it has a color. What is its trajectory?

- Do the same for your other leg, noticing if it's identical or has a different quality.

- Draw a line from your belly up your midline to your head. How do you know that is your midline? What inside you knows that this place is neither right nor left? What is the relationship of this line to your spine? Your ribs?

- From your neck, draw a line down your right arm and then your left.

- Can you see all five lines at the same time? Imagine for a moment that you could take an inner snapshot of this map of yourself. Maybe at this point it's just a stick figure. Maybe you see qualities or aspects that you hadn't noticed before.

Beginning the process of mapping your self-image begins with recognizing the literal "shape you are in" right now. It is your baseline, or starting point, for investigation. You can't transform something if you don't know what it is! You may want to take a moment and actually draw what you saw. Or write down your impressions. As you go through the book, you will see how this brain/body communication evolves.

Many systems of psychology and personal development offer archetypal studies, providing a wealth of opportunities for growth. Any one of them can open a door to personal growth and self-knowledge. The warrior, teacher, healer, and visionary offer a lens in the multifaceted prism of our existence. They manifest four essential qualities that are needed right now: courage, wisdom, healing, and vision. Let the adventure begin!

CHAPTER 2

The Warrior
Center of Presence: Pelvis

Qualities: Power, Attention, Honor

There is a scene in the 1956 Japanese film Samurai III where the greatest samurai in history sits in a room, bored, catching flies with his chopsticks. Onlookers are dazzled, but at this point in his life, skill and winning battles have become irrelevant. He questions his role as a warrior. I remember watching that scene; the warrior accomplishing an apparently impossible feat but no longer caring, no longer wanting to win another contest. He ultimately had to learn the real war was with himself, his own self-image, and what was important in his life. Being a warrior is not just knowing how to wield a weapon.

So what is a warrior, and why would you want warrior qualities? With violence raging around the planet, the stereotypical "warrior as hero" image has become complicated. Weary soldiers come home to a country unappreciative of their sacrifice. So called "warriors" commit genocide for their war lords or for personal gain. There is a difference between a mercenary and a hero, between those who use violence to oppress and those who stand up for human dignity. Warriors don't always need to wield weapons: they bring power, strength, and honor to the battle. Wherever there is corruption, oppression, or greed, there are warriors who rise up to lead revolutions, protests, and change. The battlefield can be anything from a board room or a football stadium to a hospital. Whether it's fighting climate change, kneeling in solidarity against racism, or protesting child marriage, a warrior leads by example.

This kind of warrior has always been with us, with or without weapons. There is a Native American tale called The Warrior Maiden, which goes like this: Besieged by an enemy tribe, the Oneida were starving in the hills. A girl named Aliquipiso stepped forward with a plan to lure the enemy to their destruction. She wandered into her ransacked village, where the enemy had set up camp, pretending she was lost. They captured her and began to torture her. "Oh, oh, I give up," she cried, "I will lead you to my people." She led them to a cliff. The tribe was hidden, waiting above. As soon as the enemy was underneath the cliff, the tribe rained boulders, destroying the invaders. Aliquipiso sacrificed her life as a warrior for her people. Moses, Gandhi, and Chief Seattle, to name a few great leaders, used the power of the warrior to save their people. Battles are not always about territory. Inspiration surrounds us in the form of people ranging from Harriet Tubman to Rosa Parks; people who have stood up, shown up, and led the way.

While we enjoy watching fantasies like the Avengers, or reading the exploits of mythological heroes, the call to arms in our daily life can look quite different. It may take the form of facing personal monsters that keep you from realizing your dreams. Or speaking up about what you need in a relationship. Perhaps you need the warrior energy in order to write that book. Or to quit that job. Embracing the warrior archetype means stepping into your own personal power. Of course, that in itself can be terrifying because it means you have to take responsibility for your actions. As long as you hide your light, as long as you stay small, you don't have to risk failure, ridicule, rejection, or, ironically, success.

Going Deeper

Who are the warriors you admire—what is
it about them that speaks to you?

Are there warriors in your circle of family and friends?

What do you admire/hate about them?

Is there a warrior in you? How do you feel when you hear that question?

The Warrior's Center of Presence – The Pelvis

The warrior needs to be grounded yet ready for action; to be able to sense in all directions, to know what's necessary. There is no room for contradictory signals, second-guessing or excuses. A warrior needs to be able to move in whatever direction is necessary without hesitation, including

YOU'VE GOT THE POWER!

backward. This is why martial artists learn grounding and movement exercises that focus on a grounded and mobile pelvis.

The pelvis is the geographical center of your body. It links the spine and limbs for effective action. The sacrum, which is the bottom of your spine, connects the two sides of the pelvis like the keystone of an arch. The word sacrum actually comes from the Latin word for sacred, which can be traced back to ancient Egyptian mythology. It was believed that because of its hardness and location, it protects the genitalia, making it sacred, the source of life. The sacrum receives the impact of the ground forces under your feet and conducts it up the spine. Some traditions have a name for the energy—*chi* and *kundalini* are examples—moving up the spine from the sacrum and into the rest of the self.

Since the pelvis contains and protects your organs of digestion and elimination and your reproductive organs, it is also the center of your primal emotions: terror, lust, ecstasy. It powers fight, flight, and freeze. Your psoas muscle, which runs from the lumbar spine through your hips to your legs, is sometimes called the "fear muscle." It interacts with your entire nervous system, sending you into flight, freezing you in terror, and conversely, when relaxed, allowing you to have a satisfying orgasm.[iii]

The Japanese term *Hara* refers to the lower abdominal region. Chinese traditions of Tai Chi, Qi Gong, and acupuncture locate the *dantian* or *tanden*, one of the energy centers, a little below the belly button. According to Hindu tradition, the pelvis contains the first and second *chakras*. There are varying interpretations as to the exact location of these *chakras*, but the most common locate the first *chakra* at the bottom of the pelvic floor. It connects with the legs, grounding the warrior, supporting the entire organism. The second *chakra* is located in the area of your lower colon and reproductive organs. It governs controlling/holding and letting go, spontaneity and compulsion, creativity and stagnation.

18

Without the power of the pelvis, you wouldn't go anywhere. The legs literally begin inside the pelvis, in your hip joints, which are propelled by the pelvis's several planes of motion. Because of this deep association of the pelvis with "lower" impulses, many cultures have inhibited the natural movement of the pelvis, effectively freezing the natural design of the human skeleton. Combining this lack of mobility with a society that sits for up to ten hours a day has compressed the spine and immobilized the power center. It's not simply a matter of "loosening up." You need to engage the pelvis in order to achieve dynamic stability, which is essential for knowing when to run and when to stand strong. The warrior's center of presence delivers that power.

Connecting with Your Power Center

I have worked with hundreds of people who have been shocked to discover their disconnection from the pelvic region. Years of sitting in school rooms, cars, and in front of computers have compressed the spine, effectively immobilizing the pelvis. In many societies, there are cultural taboos about pelvic movement. Allowing the pelvis to sway could label you as a loose woman, an effeminate man, a member of an inferior class (just imagine the Queen freely moving from the pelvis!). In the 60's people adored and vilified Elvis, even calling him Elvis the Pelvis because he flouted the mores of polite society. When people only associate pelvic movement with dancing or sex, there can be problems with both.

Back pain, pelvic floor issues, balance problems, and more can result from this disconnect with your center. That doesn't mean you have to learn the merengue in order to feel your pelvis. There are a myriad ways to move your pelvis as you walk through life. If you can only move one way, your movement choices are limited. This limitation then extends to your life choices. Once you experience the possibility of freedom of movement, you may discover that your life offers new options.

"The truly important learning is to be able to do the thing you already know in another way. The more ways you have to do the things you know, the freer is your choice. And the freer your choice, the more you're a human being." — Moshe Feldenkrais

- Stand up. Turn your attention to your belly. As you inhale and exhale, the belly moves. At about three-fingers width down from your belly button is the location of your *dantian*, near your second *chakra*, the center of your *hara*, as well as the very center of your body.

- Remember the lines you drew in Chapter 1? See if you can picture them now emanating from this *dantian*.

- With your hands, form a triangle: the two thumbs touching and the two index fingers touching. Put this hand triangle on your lower belly, your thumbs across your *dantian*.

- Expand your lower belly to push against your hands and release. How do you choose to expand? With an inhale? An exhale? Or simply by using your abdominal muscles? Try a little of each, see which one you prefer.

- Leaving your hands relaxed on the belly, can you shift your pelvis forward to press into your hands, and then back to the original place? What do you experience as you move forward?

- Pause a moment.

- Push your pelvis lightly against your hands, lift your heels slightly off the floor, and then drop your heels to the floor. Don't lift high, but allow yourself to feel yourself land, yielding to gravity. You will feel how the ground meets your skeleton, moving up to your *dantian*.

- Repeat this a few times.

- Walk around and notice the sensations in your feet, your posture, your belly. Whatever you experience, you are enriching your brain's sensory map of yourself.

20

- Can you walk and sense the lines still emanating from your *dantian*? The more you know, the more you know!

Going Deeper

What's the sensation in your lower belly when
you turn your attention there?

What attracted your attention the most as you did the above exercise—
the imagining, the sensation, your breath? Your movement?

How did it feel when you were done?

Those Deep Feelings

I was once at a training, and the instruction was simply for one practitioner to gently place their hand on the sacrum of the recipient. I was the recipient. I was lying on my side, and my partner lightly placed her hand against my sacrum. No pressure, no suggestion. Just her hand, holding the space. An image of my father flipping me onto my hands and knees and walloping my butt with his belt flashed across my mind. I could feel the muscles in my buttocks grab around the Sacro-iliac (SI) joint as a strange sensation flowed from that center down my legs. I recognized it instantly: shame. I broke out into a sweat (that was the closest I could come to tears in such a public space) and shuddered. I had been holding the shame of my father's anger in my butt for forty years.

People talk about muscle memory, that experiences are retained in your muscles. While there is evidence that some nuclei of the cells in your muscles remain in your muscles even when you've stopped working out and possibly reawaken when you get back in your routine[iv], these nuclei don't hold your personal memories. It's not your muscles, it's your brain and nervous system telling those muscles to contract or relax. The nervous system triggers those same anxiety/grief/shame impulses till they become a part of who you are. Digestive issues, struggles with intimacy, lower back pain, and so much more roil around with buried primal emotional stories. There is a reason we have the expression, "I was so afraid/excited I nearly peed my pants." Powerful moments affect our bodily functions as the system assesses the need to fight/flee/freeze. And these three reactions can remain stored, contracting the psoas muscle, impacting the pelvic floor, leading to physical and emotional challenges.

Going Deeper

What's going on down there? Do you have digestive/elimination issues? Pelvic floor challenges? Lower back pain? Hip joint pain?

Could any of these be connected to emotional challenges you have experienced? For now, even if it doesn't make sense, just write down what comes up for you—it doesn't have to feel connected. You don't have to make a linear assessment. Just note what comes up as you sense your pelvic region.

"You have the energy of the sun in you,
but you keep knotting it up at the base of your spine."

Rumi

Who Me? A Warrior? No Way!

I hear this all the time. It's so much easier to be small, to think small, to hide in the background, and then feel resentment or admiration for those who risk. You don't have to be a revolutionary or a hero to connect with the warrior energy within yourself. Sometimes it's about simply speaking up about what you need or having the courage to question someone's judgment. Sometimes it's about being brave enough to confront things about yourself that you have lacked the courage to acknowledge.

Ever since I was a little girl, I loved to write. Stories, poems; I just loved words. But it seemed I always said the wrong thing. Shut up, you have no right to say anything about this was like a mantra in my house. Even articles I wrote for the school paper were censored. (Granted it WAS a Catholic High School, and I was writing articles advocating wearing love beads with our uniforms.) How this love for words got twisted into me becoming a professional mime still baffles me. I had literally silenced myself. I would tell people I was still a writer: writing my mime pieces, writing my press releases. I would write a story or a play but not finish it. Or finish a draft of a novel and submit it when it wasn't really fully realized. I couldn't seem to complete anything. I would abandon writing projects with excuses like "There are so many books/plays/movies out there; who would want to read this?" or "I never succeed at anything; why even try?" and my particular favorite, "I'm so busy! I just don't have time to write!" As I began to study how I embodied my failures, I felt little chinks breaking in the wall I had constructed around my unavowed dreams. I realized that the literal core of all my excuses was fear: of not being good enough, of being irrelevant, of being mocked by my parents (and I was forty years old!!!). I made a vow to get up an hour earlier every day till I finished a book. I would not allow myself breakfast or any distraction. I would sit there for an hour, even if nothing came out of my pen. What emerged was my first book, What Are You Afraid Of? When I finally finished it (it took almost three years!) I was going to have to now SUBMIT it. More procrastination. More excuses. Then I looked at the title of my book and laughed. "Good Lord! All you have to lose is some time and paper!" I began the process of sending out the manuscript. I had no agent. No contacts. At a dinner party, I found myself seated next to a stranger. "What do you do?" "I'm an editor at a publishing company." "Really." I gulped. Flushed. Smiled. "I just wrote a book." That long pause. You know he's heard this a thousand times. "What's the title?" "What Are You Afraid of?" He looked at me strangely and said, "Send it to me."

The rest is history (at least my version of it), but I often wonder if he was moved to read my manuscript because somehow, the universe had finally acknowledged that I had stepped up to claim my rightful place.

Often, even when you have made a decision to step up, show up, and stand your ground, the feeling in the pit of the stomach, or worse yet, the chatter in your head tells you you don't deserve this, it's not going to work, who's going to listen to you. It can be overwhelming and cause a misery-inducing retreat. This is where the process of embodiment can be so helpful.

A few years ago, there was a lot of buzz about power posing: taking a posture that apparently instills a level of confidence in people. The pose looks something like the Jolly Green Giant or the vintage Superman cartoons: legs slightly apart, hands on hips, chest out. After all, we all know people with caved-in chests are wimps! But there are so many factors that might sabotage this power pose. Chest out too much, makes you unbalanced, even aggressive, and creates tension in the lower back. Not great for a superhero. Not to mention how that might compromise the breath. Stomach too tight. Legs wobbly. How do you know when you've "got it?"

It's a great pose, but if you took that pose in a meeting, people would possibly wonder about you. Unless of course, you are auditioning for said Jolly Green Giant. The idea is sound—choose a stance, a posture, a way of being that invites a different experience of yourself. By intentionally interrupting your habitual way of standing, you are sending new information to your brain, and this is the beginning of creating choice for yourself.

However, just taking a pose doesn't mean you are embodying it. In fact, it can feel very uncomfortable. If you've ever had to dress for an event in clothes that are not your style, you know how it feels to be stuck in let's say high heels or a tuxedo. Putting on an attitude can feel fake, or awkward, because your brain has a conflict between this new posture and your perceived self-image. Just because you have the positions, doesn't mean your nervous system has agreed. Faking it till you make it means you have to practice. That is why it's more effective to take things slowly, and do "try this at home." We will explore more about the power of making your own stance in Chapter 11.

Activating Your Power Center

"Don't try to lessen yourself for the world; let the world catch up to you." — Beyonce

There are many exercises that can bring you to dynamic stability: the ability to move when and where needed and to stand your ground when strength is needed. Even if you feel you don't have a warrior in you, you will find that there are moments in life when you need to "gird your loins" (did you know this saying came from ancient Greeks literally wrapping their *togas* between their legs to be able to run into battle?) and jump into the fray. If you find yourself needing to connect with your power center before a meeting, an audition, a first date, or just to get out the door in the morning, try one of these to awaken your warrior presence.

A. Learning from Lions.

As lions roar, their mouth opens wide, their torso expands, and of course, they are exhaling. Your jaw is connected to your pelvis, skeletally, muscularly, and neurologically. The movement of your diaphragm while breathing influences your pelvic floor. This simple movement sequence helps you line everything up so you can step into your power.

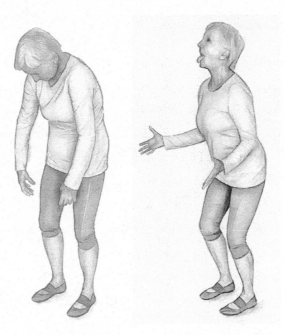

- Stand about 4–6 inches away from the wall.

- Soften your knees and direct the tip of your tailbone backward to touch the wall.

- Push your belly out.

- As you do that, open your arms, look up (maybe the back of your head will also touch the wall), open your mouth, and exhale.

- Then reverse the movement.

- Tuck in your pelvis, pull the belly in, round your back. Feel free to let your lower back connect with the wall. Lower your head and inhale as if you were drawing energy into your *dantian*.

- Try this movement slowly several times. You don't have to make it big to be effective.

- Feel free to add sound (go ahead and roar!), and for extra credit, stick out your tongue as you exhale. Believe it or not, your tongue muscles are linked to your pelvis!

B. Mobility and Stability

I highly recommend that the first time you try this exercise, you do it lying down and begin with the scan mentioned in Chapter One. If you can't lie down, you can sit with your back against the chair back or standing against the wall. You can even do it right now as you're reading. Practice now, and then when you find yourself in a life situation wherein you need to access your pelvic center of presence, you've got a clear somatic sense of the process. Your nervous system often can't differentiate between stepping into a job interview and stepping into a lion's den. When you need to stand your ground, enter the fray, or beat a retreat, you need to free your pelvis and the surrounding muscles so that you are ready.

I can't tell you how many times I've stood outside a room before a meeting or backstage before a presentation and done this against a wall right before stepping in. This simple movement will give you time to pause, reflect, and sense how your pelvis organizes your whole self, giving you that extra burst of inner strength. If you decide to just take time to acquaint yourself with the potential of moving from the pelvis, this exercise will ground and center you while relieving tension in the back.

- Whether you are lying, sitting, or standing, imagine that the back of your pelvis is against a clock face.

- If you are lying down, bend your knees and put your feet flat on the floor about hip-width apart.

- Picture the twelve numbers of the clock circling around your pelvis

- Begin to move your pelvis so that you can press it against each number. You can do this however you like: touching one number at a time, each time returning to center, or moving in a smooth circle as if you were following the sweeping second hand around the clock. Or perhaps you might want to try going a few numbers at a time and then returning.

- Try reversing your circle. Play around. Allow yourself to use whatever surface you are against to support you and allow the rest of you to just respond to the movement.

- Keep your legs relaxed if you are standing and make the other parts of yourself let go as much as feels good to you. Remember, your pelvis is connected to everything else, so your head, your shoulders, and your legs can all respond.

- Then enter that meeting, or start writing that novel and see what happens!

Going Deeper

Where in your life do you need to access the warrior's presence?

What is your sense of your pelvis as you walk?

How has your history impacted your own experience of dynamic stability?

Are you willing to show up, take a stand, and walk your talk?

Words of Power

"The single most powerful thing I can be is to be myself."
–Dwayne Johnson

One of the most famous calls to action in modern society was the slogan in the Nike ad: "Just do it." Joseph Biden used his own version in his campaign speeches: "Let's do this." Every Star Trek captain has had his and her own call to action, from "Engage," to, yes, "Do it!" What will be yours? When you need that extra ounce of initiative to take that energy of the sun burning at the base of your spine and send it out into the universe, what will you say to yourself? Some of my favorites are:

I've got this!

Yes, I can! (After all it worked for Barack Obama!)

I have the power.

The universe is with me every step of the way.

There is an alchemical power to declaring an affirmation, or an aim, that is not just some New Age idea. More than a hundred years ago, the teacher G.I. Gurdjieff told his students, ". . . take a piece of paper and write your aim on it. Make this paper your God. Everything else is nothing. Take it out of your pocket and read it constantly, every day. In this way it becomes part of you, at first theoretically, later actually."

Try it. As the immortal James Brown said, "You've got the power."

CHAPTER 3

The Teacher
Center of Presence: The Chest

Qualities: Wisdom, Responsiveness, Skill, Communication

What Do You Know?

"If I'm remembered 100 years from now, I hope it will be not for looks but for books." – Dolly Parton, creator of the Imagination Library (yes, that Dolly Parton).

I was a problem in school. I suppose if I were a child now, I'd have been diagnosed with ADD, or maybe on the spectrum, and medicated appropriately. I only remember a few things I did to merit the punishments that were meted out (including spending most of second grade in a corner at the back of the room by the lockers). But apparently, I was good at reading. And in third grade, Sister Giovanni, by far the cruelest "punisher" of all my grade school teachers, became my savior. She sent me to tutor a first grader in reading. Although her objective was being free of my apparent antics, she offered me the beginning of my lifelong love of teaching. The experience of being "of service," of having something to share, and of receiving someone's gratitude were impressions that have lasted a lifetime.

When we are called to teach, we immediately are called to learn. I often tell my students that I teach what I need to learn. The teacher needs to receive as well as give—whether it's a compliment or a criticism. Teachers are always essaying the dual roles of mentor and mentee. In Homer's epic poem, Mentor was Ulysses's friend and advisor. When gods needed to guide Ulysses and his family, they would disguise themselves as Mentor to give advice. The teacher is not always in a classroom and sometimes doesn't even have to speak in order to embody the archetypal qualities that help others learn. Knowing how to listen and breathe with another are ways to teach without lecturing.

Sometimes the Mentor is obvious: we recognize the wisdom of an elder or spiritual leader. Sometimes, however, it is the wisdom of the fool, the trickster, or the clown that offers the "growth experience." There is a Sufi folk hero named Mullah Nasiruddin, whose countless misadventures offer us a different lens for learning.

One evening a passerby saw the Mullah looking down at the ground under a streetlamp. "What are you doing, Mullah?" he asked.

"Looking for my glasses."

"Where did you drop them?"

"Across the street."

"Then why are you looking here?"

"The light is better," replied the Mullah

Like the Mullah, we often look in the wrong places for our answers. If we are lucky, we learn something that helps us gain wisdom in the process. Real learning comes from our mistakes.ᵛ After all, if you already know, what is there to learn? Current research suggests that learning actually comes from repeated errors; whether it's looking in the wrong place, hitting the brake instead of the clutch as you are learning to drive, or missing the basket as you practice your foul shots.

Students will often say to me, "I have nothing to teach," or "I can't teach." Yet you are teaching all the time. You teach by example. People around you are constantly taking in information from how you talk, walk, and even how you breathe. Each time you speak, you are teaching, because you are making choices on how to respond to a situation. Your posture is a teacher: whether you carry yourself with dignity and grace or shrink and cower at every turn. By being willing to listen and respond, you accumulate wisdom. Whether you get up in front of a classroom, listen to your child with compassion, or hold forth on your political opinion, you are embodying aspects of the teacher archetype. You certainly don't have to be in a classroom to be a teacher.

Going Deeper

Who are the teachers you admire—what is
it about them that speaks to you?

What teachers have influenced you in your life—for better or worse?

What lessons did you learn from them?

What do you have to teach others?

What are you still needing to learn?

The Teacher's Center – The Chest

I often think of the human chest as a treasure chest. Locked beneath the ribs are major organs, as well as keys to our emotional expression. The teacher listens and responds, with compassion and wisdom or with judgment and criticism.

Ancient traditions also refer to centers in the chest. Chinese tradition places the middle *dantian* in the center of the chest, governing the heart, lungs, and upper abdomen. The third *chakra* is in the region of the solar plexus, a group of nerve ganglia that are in constant communication with the question, "How are you doing?" The nerve fibers of the solar plexus interact with your vagus nerve, which is the largest nerve in your body, connecting all your major organs: your kidneys, digestive system, liver, pancreas, etc.[vi] When you have a "gut" feeling, it's coming from this complex communication that includes the solar plexus.

Your solar plexus area is a first responder for telling you what you want to feel. That feeling in your stomach when you hear you sold the novel? That jolt in your center when you realize you blew an appointment, or failed an exam, or accidentally deleted your hard drive? This connection between your solar plexus, vagus nerve, and nervous system governs your will and your wish, your reaction to success or failure. It sends chemicals to all your organs and your brain to tell you how to smile, cry, hug, run, or yell. When you "vent your spleen" or "can't stomach that person," you are directly reacting to the sensations in your gut. The gut-brain highway connects how your viscera affect your thinking and feeling.

The chest also contains the heart and lungs, two key organs for processing information and regulating our responses. Even the most allopathic medical traditions are beginning to acknowledge the relationship of the heart to the emotions. Measuring heart rate variability (HRV) makes the connection between your heart and stress, anxiety and depression vs. well-being.[vii]

Taoist tradition places the middle *dantian* in between the upper chest and solar plexus; the center of Qi, the life force that comes from our exchange of food, air, and energy toward the expression of "open-heartedness" and compassion. The fourth *chakra* is often called the heart *chakra*, but it really encompasses both the heart and lungs.

These two organs work closely together to regulate the information coming in from the outer world. Every breath you take tells your nervous system a story. This information combines with the inner sensations coming from your organs.

Your heart has neurons that communicate with your brain. Researchers are even proposing that this heart/brain participates in regulating your perception of pain, including emotional and other reactions.[viii] This is where we get terms like "emotional intelligence," and "knowing it in your heart." The lungs and heart are intimately connected: each breath you take oxygenates your blood, and your heart pumps in concert with the rhythm of your breath. This internal symphony can be beautiful or chaotic, depending on the quality of the breath. The words inspire, aspire, conspire—they all come from the original Latin word respire, which actually has its roots in the Latin word for spirit: spiritus. Inspire: to breathe in, aspire: to breathe toward, conspire: to breathe together.

The ability to sense what is taking place inside of yourself, from sensing functions like your breath or the beating of your heart to recognizing emotional reactions and stories, is called *interoception*. The teacher listens and responds to what is happening outside by sensing what is inside. Words and life situations trigger the chemical cascade we call emotions. By accessing the sensations in the chest, the teacher can regulate their response as well as understand the response in others.

How the teacher "breathes" in information, whether in the words of others, assessing a situation or, accessing their own interoceptive experience, involves listening to the quality of the breath, sensing the heart, and attending to the story the brain manufactures. The words the teacher offers come from the heart, on an exhale, exiting through the fifth *chakra*, the throat, as either wisdom or vitriol.

Your ribs surround the entire complex, connecting at the back with your spine and at the front with your sternum. We call it a rib cage, but it is less a prison than a container that encloses and supports your tender organs. If the bones of the ribs are like the walls of a castle, the rib (intercostal) muscles are like the guardians at the gate. When they are relaxed and supple, the entire wisdom center can give and receive. When the muscles are tight, the chest becomes rigid and impenetrable. The famous (or infamous) psychologist Wilhelm Reich coined the term "emotional armor" for this area. Your posture and reactions in a situation are directly connected to the freedom or tension in your ribs and spine.

Connecting with Your Wisdom Center

There are stories of adepts being able to regulate their heartbeat or change their blood pressure. Most of those people probably don't have day jobs. Those of us living with the challenges of modern living can't spend years on a mountaintop practicing esoteric exercises. But you can still use the breath to regulate your emotions and support your health. The most direct way to begin is to simply study the breath. When you inhale through your nose, air typically moves through your nose to the back of your palate, down your windpipe and bronchi into the bronchioles, which look like tree branches, to the alveoli. (Mouth breathing bypasses the palate and has been shown to be a less healthy choice.) As the lungs expand, your diaphragm moves down, and your ribs expand in all directions. The diaphragm moving downward pushes on organs, giving you an internal massage and message. And as it moves up, it does the same to the heart, while helping your lungs push air out. It's really a little miracle.

Go to any meditation retreat, and you will eventually hear guidance to "breathe in peace, breathe out love," or "breathe in love, breathe out fear." You will be guided to connect with your "heart center" and find the "peace within." And while the power of suggestion is not to be denied, what exactly are you doing? Is it simply imagination? Are you really breathing love?

We think of the air we breathe as chemistry, inhaling oxygen, nitrogen, and some trace chemicals and exhaling carbon dioxide, more nitrogen, etc. But what if you really are breathing in something more subtle? Our language is filled with the intuition that breath is more than simply dry science. "She was like a breath of fresh air." "He took a moment to breathe in what they had said." What if breath carries information that goes beyond words?

The act of breathing is intimately connected with your emotional responses to your environment as well as your inner state. For millenniums, sages have spoken about the relationship of the breath to the emotions. It's often too subtle for us to notice, but big reactions can help us recognize some breath patterns related to emotions: a gasp of surprise, holding the breath in terror, a pitiful or exasperated sigh. The breath expresses emotions with sound: wailing with grief, growling in rage, softly moaning in ecstasy.

Entire books have been written about the breath (you can find some suggestions in the index). For now, you can begin to acquaint yourself with your relationship to your breath. As you've been reading, it's likely that you've already begun to pay attention to your own breathing. And maybe you've judged it, and even found yourself unintentionally adjusting it to be "deeper". We have been bombarded by the media talking about taking deep breaths—but as you can see, breath has many options.

The good news is, you are reading this, so you must be doing something right, because you must be breathing. If air is indeed information, and how you breathe affects how you take that information in, you can begin to explore the choices you make habitually, and deepen your understanding of your own life choices so you can apply wisdom to your internal state as well as how you move through life.

The following exercises can help you tap your teacher qualities by connecting your breath with well-being and your emotions.

A. Waiting to Inhale

You can sit or lie down for this exploration. Your orientation affects where you feel movement, but the learning can take place no matter where you are. Take a moment to pay attention to how you breathe.

- Sense the length of your inhale and your exhale. Which is longer?

- Do you pause at all? Is the pause after the inhale, the exhale, or both? Which is longer? Give yourself time to explore this; don't rush to a conclusion.

- Allow your attention to expand to include sensing where you feel movement as you breathe, without judgment.

- Sense your abdomen, your lower ribs, the sides of your chest, the back of you. Don't change your breathing, just quietly notice.

- After a few minutes, try a small experiment. After you exhale, pause longer. Wait a few seconds. Then without inhaling, exhale again—you may be surprised that there is more air to exhale.

Feel free to try it more than once before inhaling. Wait until you feel your organism's natural impulse to inhale.

- Repeat a couple of times.

- Rest. Notice your breathing again.

Your lungs have the capacity to inhale and exhale about a gallon of air. But your average breath exchanges about a quart. The rest is like a layer of air that sits in reserve. You don't need a gallon with every breath. But exploring emptying your lungs in this way can help your ribs find new movement and allow the diaphragm to really move, creating more freedom in your ordinary breath. It can literally clear you out and give you some "fresh air."

There is a reason people are encouraged to breathe into a paper bag when they are panicking. Gasping in terror can bring too much oxygen in, creating a toxic reaction that makes the panic worse. I was once on a plane, and just before we began to taxi, a young woman had a panic attack. She was suddenly surrounded by flight attendants who were shouting, "Take big breaths! Breathe deeply!" Which made things even worse. It wasn't till someone suggested breathing into a bag that she calmed down. The carbon dioxide in the bag neutralized the oxygen poisoning.

B. The Breath of Impartiality

There is one breath pattern that is not (at least not yet) connected to an emotional experience. Some people call it neutral breath, zero breath, or circular breath.[ix] You may have done versions of it in a meditation class. It is not something that anyone would do habitually. It has a calming effect because there are no emotional associations with this breath. You can do this lying down or sitting. If you are sitting, sit in a symmetrical fashion, feet flat on the floor, hands quietly resting on your lap. Your eyes should be open and softly looking at your horizon. If you are lying down, you are looking at a focal point on the ceiling.

- Begin to measure the length of your inhale and the length of your exhale. Once again, notice your pauses.

- Begin to breathe so that the length of both inhale and exhale are identical. Feel free to count to yourself.

- Now change the pathway so that you inhale through the nose and exhale through the mouth. You don't have to push the air out; simply let it exit through the mouth. As you inhale through the nose and exhale through the mouth, see if you can eliminate any long pauses in between. Simply let the air circulate: in/out, in/out, as if your body was breathing you.

- After a minute or so, go back to your habitual breathing.

- Repeat.

When you are feeling stressed, emotional, or simply need to listen better, this breath provides a support for your nervous system to be centered and your thoughts and words to be impartial.

While contemporary research has shown that this breath can calm anxiety, this practice has been used for centuries. James Nestor, in his book *Breath* quotes *A Book on Breath* by Master Great Nothing, *of Sung-Shan*, from around fifteen hundred years ago: "Lie down every day, pacify your mind, cut off thoughts, and block the breath. Close your fists, inhale through your nose, and exhale through your mouth. Do not let the breathing be audible. Let it be most subtle and fine."

When you are listening, both to someone else and to yourself, you will recognize the subtle changes in your breath when it moves into your chest or tightens in the belly. These physiological events happen *before* you consciously identify that you are going into reaction, criticism, or judgment.

YOU'VE GOT THE POWER!

Yet your body already knows something is going on.[x] By sensing your breath and introducing this neutral, or as Master Great Nothing called it, "subtle" breath, you will find that not only does your attitude change, but even the situation you are in shifts. You will teach by listening.

These simple ways of experimenting with your habitual breath offer you a picture of the capacity of your lungs, as well as helping you connect with the muscles between the ribs.

By beginning to sense your breath, you can become more aware of when your breath, and therefore your emotional state, changes. Attending to your habitual breath patterns will affect how you take in the world.

Going Deeper

How did it feel to experience all the parts of you that are involved in the act of breathing?

How did attending to the breath affect your mood?

What emotions, if any, came up?

Did interrupting your habitual breath teach you anything?

Words of Wisdom

"Development is a series of rebirths." — Maria Montessori, founder of the Montessori system of education.

When we speak, we are exhaling. There are many myths and legends about how humans received language from the gods. The sound of words in any language are rooted in vibration and sound. To this day, magicians use the magic word "Abracadabra" to accompany a transformation. The actual translation of Abracadabra, from the Aramaic language, is "I have created through my speech."

During my "dark days," I was at my chiropractor's office. She asked me why I was so unhappy. "I just feel like a failure," I said. "Every project I undertake seems to go sour. I don't seem to be able to make any kind of mark on the world. I feel like such a loser." Her compassionate gaze moved me to tears.

"I want you to do something," she said. "Go home, and write the words, 'I make a difference.' Post them somewhere where you can see them—on your fridge, on your mirror. When you see those words, say them out loud.

I rolled my eyes. What a New Agey, googoo idea. I went home. "How was your chiropractic session?" asked my husband Ron. I shrugged and told him what she had said, adding some kind of sarcastic "yeah, right!" At the end of my sentence.

Ron looked at me. "Do you really feel like you don't make a difference?"

"Oh please!" I retorted.

I went to work, and a few hours later, when I returned, posted on the door was a sign. You Make A Difference. I laughed. On my closet door, there it was again. You Make a Difference. On my mirror. Above the toilet. Everywhere I turned, the sign was there. Tears welled up.

The phone rang. It was a dancer calling me to help her with a choreography issue. We worked through the problem.

"Thank you so much! I can't tell you how much you make a difference in my life!"

"What did you say?" I gasped.

She repeated it.

"Did Ron tell you to call me?" I was suspicious.

"No! I haven't talked to Ron in ages! Why?"

"Never mind."

After that, I never doubted the power of the word.

What words do you need to hear? To say? To learn? While I could fill this book with inspirational quotes, why not give yourself a moment to feel in your heart, to breathe in the words that you'd like to print up and leave all over the house.

Try it. It will make a difference.

> *"Words are sacred. If you get the right ones in the right order you can nudge the world a little."* – Tom Stoppard

CHAPTER 4

The Healer
Center of Presence: The Hands

Qualities: Energy,
Connection, Sensation

One of the great sagas in the tales of King Arthur is the story of the Holy Grail. The term "Holy Grail" has come to mean the realization of your dreams, your ultimate achievement. According to legend, it was the cup or bowl Jesus drank out of at the Last Supper. Among other things, it supposedly had the power to heal all wounds. In one version of the tale, Parsifal was one of the knights of the round table, known for his purity and simplicity. While all of the other knights tried and failed to find the Holy Grail, Parsifal kept searching. He finally encountered a magnificent castle, filled with beautiful women, fine food, and opulent furnishings, where he was invited to dine with the king, named Amfortas. Amfortas was carried in on a litter, obviously suffering from some kind of illness or wound. The Holy Grail appeared, floating past the King. All Parsifal needed to do was to ask Amfortas about his wound, and the Grail would heal him, granting Parisfal the sacred chalice. But Parsifal had been raised not to be rude, so he pretended he didn't notice the king's suffering. When he realized his mistake, it was too late: the castle, the food, the women, everything was gone.

Everyone has wounds. They are part of the human experience. Some wounds heal and are forgotten. Others leave a scar as a reminder. What is your wound?

I was about ten, running and playing during recess. I lost my balance and fell on the blacktop. Children were running all over the place, and Mark Carlton, one of the cool kids, accidentally stepped on my hand, scraping the skin by my knuckles to the bone. As I clutched my hand, he called me a klutz instead of showing remorse or compassion. Throughout the rest of grammar school, I would sometimes look at him and move my fingers across my scar, feeling the burning rage and resentment for his attitude, and the sense of shame that I had fallen in front of my peers. The scar is still on my hand, sixty years later. Now it symbolizes my resilience, my ability to get back up.

Sometimes the wounds fester, like Amfortas's wound. Often, they are hidden, sometimes on purpose (*I can't let them hurt me again*), sometimes buried so deep there isn't even a memory. These wounds block the path to your personal Holy Grail. The wound sometimes hides because it would literally open a Pandora's box of pain and sorrow. Sometimes it manifests physically: a frozen shoulder, a digestive disorder, chronic fatigue. Sometimes these symptoms are the result of an old wound, sometimes they appear to keep you from seeing something deeper about yourself, about your possibilities. And sometimes, what seems like a huge wound, upon examination, is nothing at all.

Healing the Past

I was teaching the healer segment in a training session, and after one of the lessons, a student wrote to me. "For my whole life, I have felt like a failure, that I can't do anything right. I blamed it on my father. I had a memory of doing something unforgivable, of abandoning my baby sister on the beach and of being severely punished. In my memory, I had gone off somewhere, and my parents had discovered the baby alone after searching everywhere. I felt that failure each time I fell short: I can't do anything right. In class the other day, I suddenly remembered the truth of the event. I was seven, and playing on the beach with my baby sister. My parents called us to go home. I got up and ran to them. My father turned and said, "Hey, you forgot Katy!" That was it. No abandonment. No punishment. I had completely manufactured my parents' judgment, my failure, everything! My child mind had turned this tiny event into a trauma I've been carrying around for fifty years, and it wasn't even real!"

Of course, it might as well have been real, because we make our memories real, and they can heal or destroy us.

The healer understands that we are energy, *prana*, *Qi*, or as the great astrophysicist/mystic David Bohm said, "frozen light." The uncountable dancing atoms that form the human body are a universe in themselves. The healer offers connection, sensation, and love to soothe our fragmented selves, healing not just the individual but the collective.

Going Deeper

What is your wound? What needs to be healed?

What is your Holy Grail? If you don't have one yet,
can you name something you dream about?

How have your hidden wounds, real or otherwise,
kept you from realizing your dreams?

Where do you need to be touched?

The Healer's Center – The Hands

Ask any bodyworker whether they feel there is a relationship between the quality of their touch and the response of the client, and you will inevitably get a "well, yeah!" The laying on of hands is as ancient as humanity. Naomi Kantjuriny, an Aboriginal *ngangkari* (healer), has said, "The touch of my hands has a healing effect. I give a firm, strong touch and remove the pain and sickness and throw it away from the sufferer."

In Chinese medicine the meridians, which are considered energy channels, end at the fingertips. Many important acupuncture points reside in your hands. If words have the power to make magic, it's the hands that execute the magic spell. Think about all the different movies you've seen and stories you've read where the wizard/witch/sorcerer/saint sent healing/fire/lightning bolts out of their hands. Maybe you remember Mickey Mouse as the Sorcerer's Apprentice!

- Hold your hands in front of you, palms facing each other, arms comfortably bent.

46

- Bring the palms close but not quite touching. Then slowly move them slightly apart and closer between ten and fifteen times.

You may eventually feel something like a tangible substance or a change of temperature between your hands. Don't worry if you don't. Like the experience of interoception mentioned earlier, sensing your hands is a practice. Tai chi and Qi gong practitioners move *qi* with the hands. Reiki practitioners, (again, *ki* is the Japanese word for energy) use this energy in their hands for their healing practice. Western science talks about charged atoms and electrical fields. The human body is loaded with electrical energy. At any given moment, the body is generating enough electricity to power a one hundred watt bulb. This gives new meaning to "being all charged up and ready to go!"

Talking With Your Hands

While your electrical field is around your whole body, your hands are what reach out to the world. They connect you to others and push apart. If you are an information symphony, your hands are the conductors. A nineteenth century teacher of oratory named Francois Delsarte spoke of the hands as a reflection of our thoughts. He didn't know that centuries later, scientists would learn that a huge portion of our brain is dedicated to our hands: their sense of touch, their functionality, and their language. Humans don't just gesture to clarify for others but to feed back to themselves. Your gestures begin a fraction of a second before your words,[xi] so that sometimes, when you lie, your gestures betray the truth. This is especially fun to observe when politicians speak. Delsarte said, "Gestures are the lightning, words the thunder." Your hands give and receive, support and protect, caress as well as slap. If you've ever had anyone sharply raise a hand, whether to stop you or slap you, you have felt the power of the hand and its gestures. That's perhaps why the phrase "talk to the hand" has become part of our culture.

You may not realize how many times a day you use your hands to soothe and support you. Rest your cheek and chin in the palm of your hand. Feel how that supportive gesture could lead to a bit of contemplation. If you caress your face with the palm of your hand and then caress your face with the back of your hand, how are those two experiences different?

"The hand is the visible part of the brain." — Immanuel Kant

Because your hand and brain are so intimately connected, you are constantly sending instant messages to your nervous system about your state. Drumming fingers and clenching fists are often strategies for releasing nervous energy or holding something in. It even happens when you are sleeping. I've had clients who wake up in the morning with indentations in their palms because they have been digging their fingernails into their palms in their sleep! By attending to what your hands are doing, you can use your hands as a calming and healing tool.

Extend an arm slightly forward and turn your palm so it is facing the ceiling, as if you were offering something. Let the hand relax. Notice how your fingers are slightly curled. Now turn the palm down. Your fingers will likely extend a bit. Go back and forth a couple of times. This relationship between flexion and extension are what help you grab, hold, release, and throw. The psychiatrist Iain McGilchrist has posited that the language center of the brain evolved out of this grasp reflex, whether to grasp an object or to grasp a concept.[xii]

Most of the time, your hands are doing your bidding without any conscious effort on your part. They gesture, grab the phone, chop the onions, hit the turn signal, literally without a second thought. These habits are wired from years of practice. At the same time, they are informing the rest of you: I am driving, I am eating. Your hands are also responding to your brain. I am angry. I am about to give a speech. I am walking down the aisle. They tremble, they clench, they sweat. Intentionally using your hands can calm your entire nervous system.

Your Healing Hand

- Allow your dominant arm to just hang by your side and sense your palm and fingertips. Is the hand open, closed, halfway between?

- Softly bring the tip of your thumb to touch the other four fingers so that the four fingers are gently surrounding the thumb.

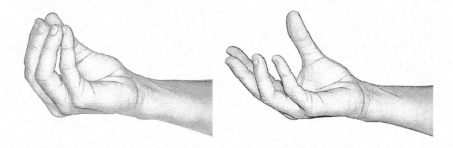

- Just as gently, release the fingers.

- Repeat this movement until your fingers and thumb find a gentle rhythm of opening and closing, like a pulse. Don't stretch your fingers, and don't squeeze them together. Leave everything really soft. I like to imagine a sea anemone, closing and opening under the water. Or picture that your closed fingers are like a bud slowly opening to a blossom.

- Once you feel you have an easy rhythm, turn your attention to your breath. Can you breathe easily as you pulse?

- You can also try it with your non-dominant hand.

This movement of the hand has many applications. Anytime you feel you are tense, anxious, or even thinking too hard, you can do this gentle hand movement to recalibrate yourself. By directing your attention to soft-ening your hand, while attending to your breath, you quiet the mind. Many people use mantras to quiet the inner chatter that sabotages their ability to think clearly and stay calm. Keeping your attention on your hand can have the same effect. Since the hand and brain are so connected, this movement can invite a similar "quiet mind." When you intentionally pulse and then suddenly notice that your hand has stopped, or has clenched, or is pulsing a mile a minute, you have instant feedback that you have gotten caught up in your emotions or thoughts. Just take a breath and resume the pulse. I can't tell you how many times I've used this movement during challenging situations. Often at tense meetings, I'll be pulsing my hand under the table. Sometimes, before a big presentation, I'm pacing backstage, pulsing both hands while staying with my breath.

Like any mindfulness practice, intentionally pulsing the hand gets easier with time. But it never becomes "second nature." It always is the result of your conscious choice to return to a centered, calm place. We will explore more applications of this deceptively simple strategy in Chapter 8.

Going Deeper

What are some of your healing activities and strategies?

How do you support healing in others?

How did pulsing your hand feel? Are there words for the sensations?

"Behold the hands, how they promise, conjure, appeal, menace, pray, supplicate, refuse, beckon, interrogate, admire, confess, cringe, instruct, command, mock and what not besides, with a variation and multiplication of variation which makes the tongue envious." – Michel de Montaigne

CHAPTER 5

The Visionary Center of Presence: The Eyes

Qualities: Insight, Foresight, Hindsight

"I have a dream that one day on the red hills of Georgia, the sons of former slaves and the sons of former slave owners will be able to sit down together at the table of brotherhood.

I have a dream that one day even the state of Mississippi, a state sweltering with the heat of injustice, sweltering with the heat of oppression, will be transformed into an oasis of freedom and justice.

I have a dream that my four little children will one day live in a nation where they will not be judged by the color of their skin but by the content of their character. I have a dream today."

– Dr. Martin Luther King

The role of the visionary can be a difficult one. Seeing possibility where impossibility reigns, visualizing the unimaginable, and providing a vision that challenges the status quo have often placed the visionary in the category of dreamer or lunatic. Envisioning what might threaten existing powers and challenge established beliefs, and looking for answers in the all the right and wrong places are hallmarks of the visionary archetype. Nikola Tesla, Preston Tucker, Giordano Bruno, even Joan of Arc (who was also a warrior!) suffered as a result of their vision. When a visionary succeeds—Nelson Mandela, Marie Curie, Steve Jobs, Maya Angelou—we elevate them, "looking up" to them.

You don't have to invent the iPhone to access the visionary archetype in yourself. To be able to see clearly is every human's birthright, even if you are blind. Helen Keller was blind and deaf, yet she used her inner vision to inspire millions of people worldwide. Insight, foresight, and hindsight are the visionary's toolbox. The visionary sees the big picture but can also focus on details, including the foreground and background of a situation. Each time you imagine your possible future, good or bad, you are using your visionary capabilities. Each time you reflect on a situation and look at all the circumstances, your visionary archetype is being called into action.

The Visionary's Center – The Eyes

Every culture recognizes the eyes as being more than rods or cones. Cultures around the world invoke protection against the "evil eye." Besides the heart, no other piece of anatomy has so many songs, films, and books dedicated to it. Almost one hundred movie titles and dozens of songs reveal the emotional power of the eyes: Lyin' Eyes, Angry Eyes, Crazy Eyes, Dancin' Eyes, and of course, Don't It Make Your Brown Eyes Blue. I have not found any songs about the pelvis yet, with the exception of a few that invite "shaking your booty."

Your eyes literally link to your thoughts. They are information receptors, taking in light, color, and shape. That information moves through your optic nerve to your brain and tells you that your husband has curly hair, the tablecloth is green, and the man standing in front of you is pulling out his wallet. When the brain misfires, we literally see reality differently. In his book *The Man Who Mistook His Wife For A Hat* Oliver Sacks told the story of a man with a disorder in his brain that caused him to see things not for what they were but as something completely different. An umbrella was mistaken for a briefcase and his wife for a hat.

Vision and perception often clash. Eye witnesses offer different accounts of the same incident: he was wearing blue jeans; no, they were black pants; it was a red car; no, it was brown, etc. Fear often causes people to literally see things that are not there, with tragic results.

Your eyes and your brain link the vast amounts of information that we call our world. As people age, and their eyesight deteriorates, their world gets literally smaller. When it becomes difficult to focus, it becomes literally difficult to focus. When peripheral vision Is impaired, the big picture starts to disappear. While age-related challenges are inevitable, there are many strategies to support the health of your eyes and broaden your view. However, you can have 20/20 vision, but if the connection to the brain is challenged, like the man who mistook his wife for a hat, your world can look very different.

The visionary sees possibility by seeing within as well as without. Insight, foresight, and hindsight are more than just metaphors. The visionary can take the long view, as well as being shortsighted and even being blindsided by a lack of vision. Clarity is important for the visionary. Because if you don't clearly see it, events can unfold in an unexpected fashion. This is one of my favorite stories of a vision gone wrong.

Several years ago, I had a student who was an up-and-coming TV producer. It was brutally hard, underpaid work, with long hours. At the same time, she had a fascination for "the glamorous life." When I would ask her, "What do you really want with your life?" she would say, "I want to be surrounded by opulence, by wealth and glamor, by a life of luxury!" Time went by. She got a job producing something; I didn't always follow her gigs and didn't know the name of the show. I knew it involved more long hours dealing with capricious celebrities. She seemed to be working 24/7 on sets in celebrity mansions, island retreats, and Manhattan penthouses, with nary a break. The host was rude and arrogant. My student cried a lot and got little sleep. She left a message for me to call the office. The receptionist answered, "Life of Luxury, how can I direct your call?" I couldn't believe that was the name of the show. She had envisioned being around a life of luxury, but had not clarified her vision: to **live** a life of luxury and not to merely be **surrounded** by a life of luxury!

Sometimes, when you clarify your vision, you realize you actually have a buried vision, something you deeply wanted that you didn't allow yourself to see.

Bettina came to me for coaching. A successful bodyworker, she said she wanted to increase her Internet presence, become an online teacher. There was a problem. Bettina hated the Internet, hated working on computers, and despised social media. It was a case of cognitive dissonance, working toward something that perhaps in the long run would be very lucrative but suffering along the way. Her confusion and misery were palpable. We did a simple movement lesson that involved using the eyes to direct movement. As her neck relaxed and eyes softened, she sighed. Then she sat up. "I don't want to be an online entrepreneur. I don't want to work my ass off building an online business. I really want, I really . . ." tears started to flow. "I just want to be a housewife. Or like a housewife. You know, have a relationship with a man I can rely on. I want to stand in my kitchen and look at my beautiful garden and cook wonderful meals. I'm tired of being alone. I'm tired of being a super businesswoman!" She had been afraid to even voice these dreams because while her career had always been successful, her love life had not. After this breakthrough event, I had some out of town engagements, and we didn't speak for a couple of months. When we finally connected, she was engaged—to a man she'd met "by chance" at a party.

Gaining Insight

Take a piece of paper, or your journal, and jot down something you'd like more clarity about in your life. Maybe it's a decision you need to make, or a challenge in a relationship. Maybe you are looking to set new goals, or trying to see your next steps in a project.

By exploring your relationship to your eyes, you change your relationship to your brain. As the eyes improve, you will see your life more clearly. This will be easier if you listen rather than read. If you are reading, you may have to read the following instructions, then put the book down in order to truly experience this.

- Close your eyes and place your hands over them so that the heels of your palms rest gently on your cheekbones and your fingers on your forehead, covering your eyes so no light comes in. There is no pressure on your eyes. Let your elbows relax, and just allow your eyes to soften in the blackness.

- Stay like that for about thirty seconds, sensing your breath.

- Observe the blackness in front of your eyes. Is it consistently black? What else appears?

- Slowly remove your hands, keeping your eyes closed. Slowly move your eyes to the right, as if you wanted to see your right ear, and return a few times.

- Pause.

- Do the same to the left.

- Cover your eyes again. Hang out in the blackness. Imagine the blackness getting even blacker.

- Remove your hands and rest with your eyes closed.

- In your mind's eye, "see" the challenge or decision you wrote about. Don't try to figure it out; just allow your inner vision to unfold the scene.

- Slowly open your eyes.

Look at your notes, and add any "insights" that have come up.

Looking Vs. Seeing

There is a difference between looking and seeing. When you are looking, your eyes are seeking, reaching out, perhaps even straining. Often when looking, I see what I want to see, or I can't see anything that I want to see! Looking means I already anticipate what I am looking for. This is useful if you are aiming a bow and arrow, focusing a camera, or chopping vegetables. But there is also the possibility of allowing your eyes to receive, to let the world come to you. In Tai chi, they call this "soft eyes," being open to receive what is happening.

- Move your eyes to the right and return a few times. How do you do it? Quickly? Slowly? Did your head want to join in?

- Now turn your head to look to the right. What did your eyes do? Likely your eyes led the way, and your head followed.

- Repeat that, sensing how your eyes lead your intention. From a functional perspective, your eyes, head, and neck like to work together. I want to *look* to my right, so the eyes head and neck execute the intention. What do you *see* on the way?

- Turn again in the same direction, but this time, keep your eyes softly centered. As you turn, allow your eyes to take in all the visual impressions: of your wall, lamp, doorknob, whatever is in front of you till you get to the same place as before. Your eyes may not be used to this. They may jump around; this is called nystagmus. It's your brain/eyes/ear canal having a confused conversation. If that happens, feel free to pause and rest, don't push it. Tension in the eyes is often invisible, part of a lifelong habit, and you can't interrupt it all at once.

- Pay attention to your breathing and just try again. Eventually, your eyes will relax.

- Repeat it a few times, and then try these experiments on the other side.

Both of these ways of using your eyes are useful for improving both your outer and inner vision. It is very interesting to play with this during your day. Periodically *look* at different things, letting your eyes lead the way to see your chair, your partner, the plant in the corner. Then other times, try the soft gaze and just let yourself *see* what's in front of you as you move around.

Clarifying Your Self-Image

In order to have foresight, one has to develop clarity. One way is to clarify the interoceptive experience, in order to "see yourself." Contemplative practices from many traditions emphasize a practice of inner vision. Some speak of an invisible third eye, which is connected with the sixth *chakra*. It's located above and between the eyes. As mentioned before, *chakras* are not just on the surface, but penetrate right through you. And yes, there is a *dantian* in the same place. Some people have connected the sixth *chakra* with the pineal gland, which even Descartes called "the seat of the soul." The pineal gland regulates our melatonin levels,[xiii] which affect our sleep cycles, so it's possible the pineal gland literally helps us *see* inside ourselves in our dreams.

Cultivating inner clarity is a time-honored process. Embarking on vision quests, consulting oracles, gazing into crystal balls or water; all these open the portal to seeing beyond our ordinary vision. Dreaming as an act of creation is part of many shamanic practices. In his book *Courageous Dreaming: Dreaming the World Into Being* shamanic teacher Alberto Villoldo calls these seers "the Earthkeepers": "we're dreaming the world into being through the very act of witnessing it."

Morpheus was the Greek God of dreaming, working in partnership with other spirits to control the sleep of humans. In the science fiction movie "The Matrix" the character named Morpheus is a visionary, responsible for "awakening" the hero out of the perpetual dream state where the human race is imprisoned, reversing the Greek myth.

Your brain is constantly communicating with all your parts. Your relationship with your parts is what some people would call your self-image: how you *see* yourself. If you are reading, read this whole next paragraph and then try it. If you prefer to be guided, you will find an audio of this meditation here:

- Find a comfortable, relaxed position. Lying down, knees bent or straight, sitting in a comfortable chair—whatever feels good.

- Close your eyes. Imagine that your eyes can look up into your skull. Feel free to let your eyes move. Your eyes move right and left as if you were scanning the inside of your head.

- Continue moving your eyes left and right as you begin to scan downward. It's as if your eyes have become your own internal MRI. It doesn't have to be fast.

- Scan back and forth, going down the inside of your face, your neck, your chest.

- As your eyes move back and forth, pay attention. Sometimes it feels like you've come to a block. Or you suddenly lose your place. Or there seems to be a different color in your mind's eye. Sometimes people become aware of tensions, or emotions. Sometimes people feel absolutely nothing. Don't strain.

- Go all the way down to your feet.

- Rest.

Going Deeper

What feelings or thoughts did you encounter
during these three explorations?

How do you *see* yourself?

What is your vision for your future?

Go back to what you wrote before the first exercise. Is
there some new insight or image you can add?

CHAPTER 6

The Dark Side

Who knows what evil lurks in the minds of men? The Shadow knows
Bwah hah hah hah!" – 1930s Radio Program, *The Shadow*

When the qualities of our four archetypes become distorted, so that their powers can be used for harm, we enter the shadow realm. The human experience is filled with challenges that go beyond mere survival. Unlike any other creature on this planet, humans make moral choices. And while different cultures have different moral codes, the four shadows are consistent in that they inflict pain: physical, mental, and emotional.

The shadow takes the power of each archetype's center of presence and uses it against others. This power is seductive and can engulf a nation. Hitler used his visionary abilities to seduce a nation to genocide. Jim Jones was a twisted teacher who led his flock to a suicide that bequeathed our culture with the term "drinking the Kool-aid."

These four archetypes do not contain all the evil in the world, because the shadow is very creative. But it can give you a portal from which to examine your own shadow. Darth Vader was a warrior who literally went to the "dark side." Growing up, I'd watch my warrior father transform from a strong, energetic hero in my eyes to a violent, terrifying beast, his shadow overtaking his nobler instincts. Maybe you can name some examples, fictional or from your own life, whose shadow influenced you. Whether all you can think of is Voldemort or your third grade teacher, write it down.

Everyone has a shadow side, a piece of themselves that they cannot or will not see. Each of the four archetypes offers a lens into aspects of our personal dark side. A friend of mine once said, "I don't trust anyone who's always sunny side up, because it means they are hiding their shadow." While it's easy to see someone else's flaws, seeing your own is like trying to find your shadow at high noon—it's obscured by the angle of your vision. And yet, as Jesus said in the Sermon on the Mount, ". . . first cast out the beam out of thine own eye; and then shalt thou see clearly to cast out the mote out of thy brother's eye."

So how do you begin to see what you can't or don't want to see? I don't know if anyone has yet found an evidence-based reason for this, but experience tells me that often the thing that I find most offensive in others is lurking in me. One way to clarify the image in the "glass darkly" is to examine your reactions to others. Strong negative reactions can often inform us about our dark side.

I have a colleague who I have known for almost thirty years. From the moment we met there was friction. As one of my trainers, she seemed to always find fault with my behavior. I on the other hand found her arrogant and egotistical. She would go out of her way to demean me in public, making cracks about my looks, or my past as a street mime. I would retort with acid comments about her supposed wit, her failed career as an actress. I often literally felt myself bristle when she entered the room as I got ready for a battle to protect my ego. Often, afterward, I felt dirty and a little sad. She had dragged me down into invective and rudeness. One day I realized, that no, this was not just about her. After all, if I wasn't as egotistical and arrogant as her, her words would have no impact on me. I would have no need to lash back or be angry. The truth was, I am just as self-important and arrogant as she. When she behaved in that manner, she triggered my dark side, a piece of myself I didn't want to see. Now, when we see each other, I keep a close monitor on the sensations in the pit of my stomach, the back of my neck. When I feel the rise up of what I've come to call Darth Lavinia, I begin a neutralizing breathing, soften my face and hope that this time, I won't fall down the dark hole of my ego.

The shadow literally blocks the light, so you can no longer see your center, your true self. As you look at the following questions, you can ask yourself if you have ever had to face these in yourself.

The Warrior: Pelvis / Centered

What happens when you've lost your center?

The Teacher: Heart / Wisdom

What happens when the heart twists?

The Healer – Hands / Healing and Light

When does a healer lose the light?

The Visionary – Eyes / Insight and Foresight

When does a visionary narrow their vision or refuse to see?

Looking Within

- Who are some people whose dark side affects you? They don't have to be famous; they can even be members of your family. It could be some of the names you wrote above. They may disgust you, make you tense, anger you. List them on a piece of paper. Sometimes, this can take some time. We often don't even want to acknowledge that a certain person or personality rubs us the wrong way. It may be a politician, or a comedian. Just write it down.

- Next to each name, write what it is about them that upsets you. It could be one simple word: greedy, mean, arrogant . . . It could be a little story: He always puts people down, and you can't get a word in edgewise. Once you have your list, take a moment to study it.

- Take another piece of paper. Write the words: When have I been . . . and finish the sentence with a quality you loathed from the first page.

When have I been . . . greedy?

When have I been . . . too quick to judge?

When have I been . . . the smartest person in the room and unwilling to listen?

You may discover that there are sides of you that you have refused to see. Don't castigate yourself. Don't deny yourself. Just allow yourself to "see."

A Peek Behind the Curtain

How often does your dark side flash at someone without your awareness? That moment of dismissal, arrogance, judgment, even hatred that is betrayed in a tilt of the head, tightened lips, neck tension? How can you begin to "see" your attitude?

- Grab a chair that has a back but no arms and turn it around. Sit astride it "cowboy style," so you can rest your arms on the back of the chair.

- Lower your head slightly. Begin reaching with your chin, down toward your hands on the back of the chair. Do it very lightly—a delicate, subtle movement.

- Then take that same movement (the impression is like a chicken pecking in very slow motion) and begin pecking as you move your head to the right, a peck at a time.

- Return and rest.

- Try the same thing to the left.

- Repeat the same sequence, but look straight ahead instead of down.

- As you move your chin, tighten your lips. Play with turning your head, pecking, tight lipped.

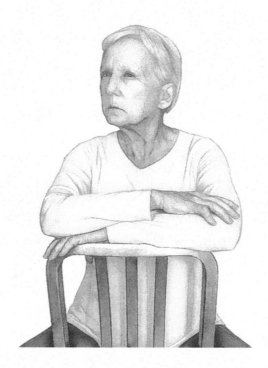

- Pause in at different moments, facing different directions, tight lipped.

- Move your eyes to one side and pause, sensing the tension in your face in this attitude.

- Try moving your eyes the other way.

- Narrow your eyes a bit. Do these adjustments slowly.

- Notice if any of these small movements and holdings evoke a sense of a familiar posture or attitude. Do they bring up situations where perhaps you've taken on a similar attitude in your head, lips, or eyes?

- Rest.

- Try moving your head backward, retreating from the back of the chair. Do it going to the sides.

- As you do, begin to play with your eyebrows. They may actually move spontaneously as your head goes back and furrow your brow a bit.

- Look to the side, head going back, and raise your eyebrows just a bit.

- Push your head back and wrinkle your nose.

- Don't rush through these. Take a moment in each configuration to ask yourself, *Have I ever taken this expression? What does it feel like?*

- Stop doing the movement. Stand up and walk around. Notice If your posture or face feel any different.

Our faces make countless micro-expressions all day long. Sometimes the expression is so fleeting, one can only catch it through slow motion playback on video. Tiny facial adjustments that betray our contempt, jealousy, resentment, judgment, arrogance, insecurity and more, below the level most people can consciously perceive. By playing with your repertoire apart from social interaction, you can begin to recognize some of your shadow attitudes and habitual expressions that affect your relationships with others and yourself.

Going Deeper

What expressions appeared on your face? What did they remind you of?

Did memories of interactions come up?

Me and My Shadow

There was a woman in my meditation group who drove me up the wall. I would say to myself, "Why do you let her get to you like that?" She always seemed to try to second guess me and was always looking for approbation from the group. Often, when a special event was planned, she and I were thrown together, and inevitably, she would say something I disagreed with. One time, she suggested something about the schedule. I thought it was a terrible idea but didn't want to react. (We are a meditation group after all, we need to be "present" with each other, right?) Before I said anything, she said, "You're judging me." "What made you say that?" I asked. "You always blink slowly when you judge me." Busted. I had unconsciously developed that habit of blinking in order to disguise the flashing in my eyes.

It's difficult to see your shadow in the moment. When you are, as G.I. Gurdjieff said, "identified" with a situation, you only see your point of view. Even when outwardly agreeing with someone, you reveal yourself to others. Dracula casts no shadow, has no reflection. He can never see himself for what he is. You do have the ability to reflect in order to catch aspects of your shadow.

Can I See That Again, Please?

There is an ancient practice described in many traditions, sometimes called recapitulation or review. It is very difficult, but incredibly valuable.

- As you lie in bed before sleeping, take three intentional breaths to clear your mind.

- Begin to visualize your day backward, as if you were playing back a movie in your mind's eye. Mentally walk backward out of your bed, back to the bathroom, etc. Keep unreeling your day, paying attention to conversations, decisions, and encounters.

The first few times you do this exercise, you'll probably fall asleep before you back out of the bathroom. (In fact, it can be a great way to cure insomnia!) But you will eventually find yourself going back further into your day. As you practice this, you will notice that there are blank spots in your vision, parts of your day where as you approach them in your mind, you drift off or find yourself thinking about something else. Take note. With practice (and it is a practice!), you will replay interactions with people and be able to see your behavior, the words you chose, your attitude in the situation. You'll want to skip over those moments where you might have been righteous, selfish, or arrogant. See if you can bear seeing your shadow with compassion. Sense what you feel in your gut and in your heart as you revisit without blinders.

The important thing to remember when working with your shadow is that you are not trying to kill or destroy it. The archetypes' shadow is part of the human experience. Deny the shadow and the balance is off. Unlike angels, humans have to struggle with an inner darkness. This struggle is what brings us closer to our true possibility.

PART II

What Is Your Kryptonite?

"Find your true weakness and surrender to it. Therein lies the path to genius. Most people spend their lives using their strengths to overcome or cover up their weaknesses. Those few who use their strengths to incorporate their weaknesses, who don't divide themselves, those people are very rare. In any generation there are a few and they lead their generation." – Moshe Feldenkrais

Superman was invulnerable, with just one weakness. When exposed to the element of kryptonite, a stone from his home planet, he lost all his superpowers. Achilles was considered the greatest Greek warrior, invulnerable with the exception of one heel. The Hindu god Ravana's egotism, his fear of failure, led to his downfall.

Unlike the shadow, which twists and corrupts the archetype's "true north," harming others, kryptonite is the quality or behavior that literally takes away the archetypes' ability to manifest in their true power. Like Achille's heel, anxiety patterns, inner chatter, self-sabotaging habits or social conditionings can keep you from realizing your dreams. Recognizing and incorporating your "weakness" will turn your liabilities into assets.

When you learn to recognize your kryptonite, and acknowledge how it's holding you back, transformation is possible. You can then take that liability and make it your asset. As you go through the next section, remember that being honest or sincere with yourself without beating yourself up is a great path to learning.

CHAPTER 7

The Warrior's Kryptonite – Fear

"What makes the elephant charge his tusk in the misty mist or the dusky dusk? What makes the muskrat guard his musk? Courage." — The Cowardly Lion, *The Wizard of Oz*

You've read enough books and seen enough movies to know that fear is an essential survival strategy. Fear pumps you with adrenaline to help you fight or flee. It shuts down your digestive system (which ironically sometimes means you suddenly have to go to the bathroom). It heightens your alertness and helps you do what you need to do to survive. You don't want to be "fearless." The Darwin Awards are a tongue-in-cheek honor bestowed posthumously annually on a list of people who lost their lives because they fearlessly did incredibly stupid things.

We're not talking about trying to talk on your cellphone on the edge of a cliff or trying to find buried treasure in the Rockies in the middle of winter. And we certainly aren't talking about having to battle wild animals or dive off that cliff into the ocean below to save your partner. Modern society has taken this brilliant survival quality and turned it against your ability to do what you want.

Fear of rejection, failure, ridicule, financial loss, abandonment, and even success may not cause the rush of adrenaline mentioned above, but they *will* become the obstacles to attaining your holy grail. Like the Cowardly Lion, you need to acknowledge your fear in order to overcome it.

So What Are You Afraid Of?

We tend to either avoid or put aside things because we don't want to look at the kind of fear that might be behind it. Take a look at the following list of questions. As you read them, you may say, "I don't know if this has anything to do with fear." But maybe it does. You can simply answer yes or no to these questions, or take some time to reflect, especially if the answer is yes.

Do people accuse you of being a workaholic?

Are you a procrastinator?

Do you often watch TV instead of doing other activities?

Do you feel under the weather more than once a week?

Do you drink or take recreational drugs more than once or twice a week?

Do you overeat?

Do little things piss you off to no end?

Do you have trouble sleeping?

Perhaps the above seem like innocuous behaviors. Watching TV or losing one's temper are part of life. It's a question of choice and habit. There are all kinds of strategies employed to cover up the discomfort of fear. Avoidance or indulgence can be two sides of the same coin: I'm overeating in order to avoid needing to look at my novel, or I'm watching TV in order to not think about how I hate my job but am afraid to quit. All of these are different choices you might make in order to soothe yourself and not step into your power.

My father's idea of teaching me to swim was to walk with me to the edge of the dock and then suddenly shove me off the dock. As I screamed and struggled, he laughed, telling me to either sink or swim. I somehow dog paddled to the shallow water. After that trauma, I always found some way to either get out of swimming or even better, end up somewhere else so I didn't even have to swim. Each time I got into the water, no matter what, within a few minutes I was out of breath and exhausted. I didn't realize that I was breathing in a panic, even when there was no reason to panic. I married a former lifeguard who adored swimming. Each time we went to the beach, I would splash around but would always say things like, "I just don't like swimming," or "I'm just not a water person." One day, my husband said, "You just don't know how to swim." I sputtered and protested and resisted. He took me to a pool and began to teach me. He celebrated when I actually swam one lap. He helped me see my fear. Now I love swimming. If it hadn't been for him, this little piece of kryptonite would have kept me from a lifetime of joy.

Take a blank piece of paper and turn it landscape-wise so that it's horizontal. Draw two lines down the paper to make three columns. On the first column, make a heading that says: "Things that I avoid."

Don't think too deeply about this; you can always come back to this, and you're going to also find new insights as time passes. Just write the first things that come into your mind: things that you don't like to do, that you avoid, that you stay away from.

For example:

I hate the water.

I avoid cooking like the plague.

I don't like it when Margaret comes to our group.

I can't stand it when I'm in a room of people I don't know.

I hate being late.

Whatever comes up for you. It might even be "I don't like the color red." Whatever comes up that falls in the category of "I don't like" or "I don't want to be near" or "I avoid," just write those down as a list. Again, you can always add to it later.

Now of course, going back to this idea of fear as being useful, there are things that we avoid that are very sensible, for most people anyway. If you say, "I avoid walking on a dark alley in the middle of the night in a strange country," that's pretty reasonable for most people. That would be a legitimate fear, and that would be something that you would avoid. There are people, of course, who enjoy that, but that's another subject!

Now, in the second column, you can write "What am I afraid of?" Look at each of the things you avoid and see if you can make a connection. You might look at "I don't like to go to parties" and your immediate response might be, "It's not because I'm afraid. I'm not afraid of parties!" But what is taking place in you emotionally as you look at the things you avoid? In the third column, write "It makes me feel . . ." Where are you feeling it in your body? If you feel like your gut says "No, it's not that I'm afraid, but they piss me off," go ahead and write that. Jot down a feeling word as you're writing your response to each of the things that you listed. These exercises can open up the related question for you. Then reflect on it later.

Notice your breath. Do you feel it in a particular part of your body as you're responding to your own dislikes and avoidances? How can you use the intelligence of your body to help you move forward? It's not like you suddenly have to start going to parties. That's not the point. Because you don't have to like going to parties. It's about having the freedom to choose from a place of presence when you admit being afraid of the water, or when you sit down in front of the blank canvas and want to start painting and acknowledge you are afraid you're not good enough. You can recognize your body's reactions.

Going Deeper

What story do you tell yourself when you reject
doing something or being with someone?

What happened when you were young that
kept you from trying something?

Finding Your Footing

The warrior's center of presence is the center of the body, the pelvic region. The root chakra at the bottom of the pelvis also includes the legs. Our legs and feet can literally "root" us, supporting us to step up or stand our ground, or freezing us, even buckling under us. We even have a saying: Feet, don't fail me now! As discussed in Chapter 2, fear can impact the hips, keeping you from moving forward. By grounding yourself from the feet up, you can reinvigorate your power center.

- Sit down, either in a chair or on the floor, and take off your shoes and socks.

- If you can reach a foot, you can put your ankle on your thigh, or you can just sit on the floor cross-legged and take a moment to take a tour.

- Using your hands, examine how your toes move. Check out your calluses, formed where you put the most weight on your feet.

- Explore your arch. The arch of your foot has muscles that go horizontally across your foot, unlike your longer muscles. These "transverse" muscles support your skeleton as well as communicate with your hips and pelvis.

- Stand up and feel how your feet contact the floor. Every step you take conducts the forces coming from the earth up through your skeleton, providing information on how "grounded" you are, what kind of surfaces you are touching, and how to mobilize the rest of yourself.

- Rise up slightly on the balls of your feet, your heels just an inch or two off the ground, and then drop down onto your heels with a thump. See if you can land on your heels in such a way that your entire body feels the vibration. Thump down.

- If you have foot or heel problems, take care to keep your movements within your comfort range. This should feel fun. Then see if you can play with rhythm, maybe two quick lifts and landings in a row, thump, thump, then a rest. Or do a few fast ones, then pause.

- Repeat this a few times.

- Take a walk around and feel how your feet contact the floor now. Is your walk different?

This activity has many applications besides grounding you. The vibration and contact with the ground can strengthen your bones as they conduct the ground force, and strong bones can help you feel strong inside. If you remember being a child having a tantrum and stomping around, you know the experience of literally discharging energy through your feet. Tension, anger, frustration, and anxiety can simply be thump, thumped right out of your bones.

When you feel that paralyzing gripping sensation in the groin that makes you want to run from opportunity, take a few minutes and play with this movement. Then add sensing your breath and your *dantian*.

Going Deeper

What is your attitude toward trying these movements? If you are resistant, where do you feel the resistance?

If you tried the exercises above, how do you feel now?

Take a look at your piece of paper. Are there any additional insights you can add?

One Step At a Time

If you are afraid of heights, you don't necessarily want to go sky diving. And if you are afraid of getting your novel rejected before you even start writing it, you don't want to start calling agents. One way to approach your fear is to explore successive approximations of things that feel safe. Step by step, you will find yourself approaching your goal without violence or force. Instead of trying to conquer your fear, make it your friend. That knot in your stomach, that catch in your breath, that clenching of your teeth—they are all somatic clues. Pause, listen, and ground yourself.

Look at your list of things you avoid/hate/fear. Pick one of them, maybe not one of the big ones. On a fresh sheet of paper, write down that one item:

I don't like it when Margaret comes to our group.

List all the reasons that pop up:

She monopolizes the conversation.

She always has something to say.

Everyone thinks she's so great.

She wears too much makeup.

Write all the emotions that come up as you write.

I feel small and unimportant around her.

I'm afraid she'll not like what I have to say.

I want to be appreciated for my contributions without having to compete with her.

I wish I knew how to apply makeup.

I wish I had the courage to dress and act so large.

As you write these things, begin to pay attention to the sensations in yourself. Where does the tension rise? When does your breath change? Take a moment to do the grounding exercise above. Then decide to do something small, something no one else might notice.

I could go to the mall and get a makeup consult.

I could walk into the meeting with a different posture.

I could listen to Margaret and sense where I feel it in my body.

Whether you are dealing with personal relationships, a phobia that inhibits your potential, or are afraid to embark on a new life journey, you can begin with small steps. Like when learning to swim, celebrate doing one lap, one small thing that brings you closer to your warrior power.

CHAPTER 8

The Teacher's Kryptonite – Ego

"Whenever I climb I am followed by a dog called ego."
— Friedrich Nietzsche

There are many interpretations of the word "ego." It can range from simply identifying "I" to labeling someone a narcissist. We all look up to those who "know" something. It's easy to give up your own authority to a guru, a professor, or a parent who convinces you that they know better.

When I was visiting a cousin in Europe many years ago, he was driving us somewhere unfamiliar. Each time his GPS launched, this mellifluous British male voice would intone, "Follow me, I know the way!" And I believed it, because he sounded so confident.

Many New Age teachers speak about "following your inner GPS." But how do you know when to trust it, and when it's taking you down a road that disappears into the woods and drives you into a river? (This actually happened to me!)

The need to be right, or the fear of being wrong, can be paralyzing. Why do we need to be right? How does it feel when we're wrong?

I grew up in a family where if I did anything wrong, incredibly creative and unpleasant punishments were meted out, which made me an expert at covering up what I did wrong. My mantra at that time was: It's not my fault. It's not my fault. Somebody else did it. It's not my fault. When I was getting ready to go to college, my father sat me down for a rare heart-to-heart talk. He said, "I want to tell you the three most important things that helped me to survive." My father was a Holocaust survivor, and he rarely talked about the war, so I was eager to hear his wisdom. "Number one: never let anybody know you don't know what you're doing. Number two: if you do something wrong or make a mistake, don't get caught. Number three: if you get caught, blame somebody else."

Stunned, I suddenly recognized my programming. It had been an invisible part of my entire childhood. However, anyone who recognizes a life behavior knows it doesn't change just because you see it. I unwittingly continued carrying this gremlin of "it's not my fault" into my adult life.

I was at a meditation retreat, and there were at least one hundred people there. I was on the lunch-serving team. The room was packed. Everybody was sitting on cushions with their legs crossed, and we were all being very careful carrying the food and placing it down for *each person. It was a sacred and silent process. Somehow the plate I was carrying slipped. And the food, which of course involved gravy and salad with dressing, landed all over this woman who was sitting in quiet meditation. Out of my mouth loudly burst, "It's not my fault." To have one hundred pairs of eyes looking at me with compassion and forgiveness as I said something so obviously untrue was one of the most amazing experiences in my life. After that, "it's not my fault" became my wake-up call. Whenever I caught myself saying "It's not my fault," I would question myself. Maybe it **was** my fault. Learning to accept my mistakes and not fear punishment has helped me become a better teacher.*

Looking stupid, not being smart enough, making mistakes, and failing are ego-bruising events. This is why we love and laugh at really great clowns. The fool takes our precious ego and lays it out for all to see. We laugh at the clown's struggle to make things right, while only making things worse. Yet we desperately try to control our world so that we never make fools of ourselves. But who are we fooling? How are we hiding behind our egos?

The Ego Triad

Criticism

We've all experienced teachers who are good at making us feel small. Whether it's a parent, professor, ballet instructor, or football coach, they put themselves above you, using their authority to disempower you. While constructive criticism helps someone to grow, using criticism as a weapon or to put oneself above another makes the teacher a tyrant. If you grew up in an atmosphere of negative feedback, it can seem impossible to see anything positive.

I was asked to teach a course on body language at the local university. Academia is not my forte, but I did my best trying to stick to a syllabus, learn to grade, and address student antics like plagiarism and "the dog ate my homework" excuses. At the end of the semester I received the student feedback form. "Didn't stick to the syllabus!" and "Unsympathetic!" leapt off the page. I was devastated. A colleague who also teaches there told me, "Hey, I heard your course was really great, congratulations!" "That's a laugh," I replied, "They hated it. The feedback was awful." I happened to still have the form in my hand, and I thrust it out to her. "Wow, what are you talking about?" she asked. "You got a 4.5 overall rating. And listen to this: 'I never thought about my body as anything more than a machine, now I'm aware of so much more.' Or this one, 'Ms. Plonka is funny and full of knowledge.' Why do you think the feedback was awful?" I grabbed the paper. She was right. My critical eyes had zeroed in on only the negative comments, and I literally had not even seen that there was positive feedback. I actually couldn't believe my eyes.

How do you disempower yourself? Criticizing is not just criticizing others but also your inner dialogue of criticizing yourself, beating yourself up. Fear of criticism can often keep you from even trying something. Criticism is not simply negative feedback. Sometimes it can appear as impatience or contempt or even anger at yourself or someone else. What would be the opposite of criticism for you? If impatience is a quality you recognize, imagine what patience with yourself and others might offer. Perhaps instead of criticism you need forgiveness or acceptance.

Judgment

"All comparisons are odious."

From Cervantes to Shakespeare, this phrase rings through our literature, attesting to a deep inner knowledge that as soon as we judge, we have lost our objectivity.

Where does judgment live in the body, in your sensations? When you are judging someone or judging yourself, where do you feel it: in the chest? the head? the eyes? When you say, "Oh, that's so stupid," where does it come from? Judgment appears in one's life in the act of comparison. "He is better than me." Or "I could have done that better than them." Judgment also divides people: I am right and you are wrong. Righteous indignation and polarized opinions don't simply change because of logical argument. Research has shown that strong opinions are actually part of the brain's wiring.[xiv] That means arguing about a hot button issue is not the path to agreement.

What about when you judge that someone's opinion has more value than yours? And that therefore you are not good enough? Dismissal is the ultimate judgment. Dismissing myself, dismissing my own feelings, dismissing somebody else.

Control

"If you want something done, you have to do it yourself." This was drummed into me as a child. When I needed help or support, I was told, "You made this mess, you get yourself out of it." I became a self-employed workaholic, trying to do everything myself. Running my business, doing my marketing, cleaning my house, maintaining my websites, even making the snacks I served at my workshops. (I still make the snacks!) My husband would watch me running myself ragged, gently suggesting I hire some help. He dubbed me Little Red Hen Productions. The Little Red Hen is a fable that is supposedly about the merits of hard work. The little red hen finds some wheat and asks for help milling the wheat, kneading the dough, and baking the bread, but in each request, no one helps her. She ends up baking and eating the bread herself. Of course, the difference between us is that she did ask for help, while I refused it in fear that if I didn't do it myself, the bread would turn out like crap.

What do you do when you feel a lack of control? What are you holding on to? Possibly it's something that you can't even see, like me holding on to that mantra of "do it yourself" that I'd received from my parents.

I have a recurring dream. I am scheduled to teach a class. As people arrive, I realize there is not enough room, and so they open another room down the hall. I try to teach in two different rooms, running from one room to the other. People start to get impatient. Some people start talking, then getting up and leaving. I can't remember which thing I said in which room. I panic as I try to keep everyone together. I desperately start yelling at people to lie down, to just wait a second, that I will get it all under control.

A primal fear we carry from childhood is of being cast out. I was constantly threatened that if I didn't behave, I would be sold to gypsies. While this made the idea of gypsies an alluring lifelong fascination (they would actually pay to have me?) for me, it also instilled in me a desperate need for acceptance. My fear of failure, and the way I tried to hold on to things was perhaps my way of trying to protect myself and stay in the tribe. If I fail, if I'm wrong, I'll be rejected, it will all be over, and I will starve to death. Or . . .

What would happen if you let go? In Chapter 3, I mentioned the fool that appears in tarot. If you look at the traditional depiction of the fool, he's stepping off the edge of a cliff. Is he oblivious? Or simply trusting that all will be well? We work too hard to not make fools out of ourselves. What if the need to control is also about fear of failure or of looking like a fool?

The essence of good comedy is someone enduring one nightmare after another. It sounds paradoxical, but we laugh at others' failures. From Charlie Chaplin to Bill Murray to Melissa McCarthy, we laugh as they try and fail: to fall at love, to eat a shoe, to fight a gopher, even to commit suicide. The humor is in the failure. We laugh when the clown falls on her face, but when we fall, or fail, we don't see the humor in it. The fear of looking like a fool, the fear of not owning my mistake: that I tripped or that I misspoke, makes me desperate to protect my precious ego.

"A person who never made a mistake has never tried anything new." — **Albert Einstein**

What is the sensation of looking like a fool? What is the chemistry of embarrassment, shame, regret, realization? In the moment of a "fail"—the proposal that gets deep sixed in a meeting or the phone call that goes badly— your body betrays you. The face flushes, sweat starts to pour down, trembling begins. When you blush, you're actually feeling not just embarrassment but energy as well. The heart is pumping, and adrenaline is stimulating you to action. Adrenaline also activates your sweat glands. Flop sweat is your body's programmed fight/flight response. It doesn't differentiate between a tiger and your failed standup comedy routine.

The teacher understands that mistakes are necessary for learning. You can take a chance and be open to the outcome. Learn to acknowledge your error without criticizing yourself, without judging.

After his presidency, a reporter asked George Bush if he could share with the reporter what he felt was the greatest mistake he had made during his presidency. Bush just sat there. He couldn't think of a single mistake that he had made in his years as president. If you can't see your mistakes, how can you learn?

Going Deeper

As you look at the above three teacher kryptonites, how do you feel?

Where do you feel it? Is it a sensation, emotion, or something else?

Can you breathe into an honest response?

Can you remember early experiences of being criticized or judged?

From your adult perspective, how did these events impact your life choices?

Where are you feeling "control issues?" What needs to be let go of?

What have you not tried because you don't want to look like a fool?

When you fail, where do you feel it in yourself?

You Teach What You Need to Learn

Once you acknowledge the pitfalls of the ego, true learning can take place. Embracing the unknown, being curious, and making mistakes without judgment or criticism can feel like a huge project. But as long as you stay in your controlled environment governed by automatic habits, you will be forever trapped by your inner critic. I can't, I'm not good enough, he gets all the breaks, will forever be your mantras.

Or you can embrace the art of letting go. Learning doesn't mean you have to go back to school, although you certainly can. Simply interrupting your habitual behavior can literally change your brain. You can embody the teacher archetype by learning something new about yourself.

It has been shown that when you interrupt your physical habits or learn a new motor skill, you think differently as well.

Some interesting things you can try:

Use your nondominant hand to brush your teeth, handle your fork, or use your mouse.

Practice juggling (I'm still working on that one!).

Walk backward a couple of times a day.

Get some modeling clay (the kind that doesn't dry out), blindfold yourself, and create a sculpture in five minutes. (If you do this five minutes a day, you'll be amazed!)

Stand on one leg when talking on the phone.

Read a book upside down.

What other ways can you introduce novelty into your life?

Teaching By Listening

There are two ways to listen. You can listen in order to reply, or you can listen in order to understand. Often we're not listening in order to understand, to really hear what someone is saying, or even listening to ourselves. Instead, even as the person is speaking, responses, judgments, commentary, and comparisons are occurring within us. The brain is busy forming defenses, rebuttals, and arguments. Even if you don't say them, they're going on in your head. With this kind of inner chatter, you really can't take in what's happening because you're lost in judgment. The teacher's center is the whole torso, the emotional part of the body, with the heart being the center of that. By listening to the sensations in the chest: the heartbeat, the quality of the breath, where there is tension in the upper back, you can begin to recognize when you are not really listening to understand yourself or others. This is the first step toward experiencing impartiality.

One way to know whether you are listening in order to reply vs. listening to understand is to monitor your breath. In Chapter 3, you explored quieting the nervous system by becoming aware of your breath and its capacity to relax you and experience impartiality with the zero breath. But your breath can actually help you to listen.

We have a breath pattern for every emotional state. These breath patterns signal the nervous system to release different chemical cocktails for dealing with life situations. Pattern 3 of the zero breath has no emotional charge, which is why it is used as a calming strategy.

There is a breath pattern that anyone can learn to help with compassionate listening. You probably spontaneously engage in this breath often, since it helps one to relax, to think more clearly, and to listen better. Adopting this breath intentionally when you need to access the compassionate teacher, or just be compassionate with yourself, is invaluable. When you are tense, it is hard to listen, and this is how misunderstandings occur. When you learn the breath sometimes called tender regard or compassionate attention, along with a specific body attitude, you will have a tool for opening your heart to yourself and others.

Tender Regard

- Sit with your feet flat on the floor, your hands resting comfortably on your lap.

- Begin to sense your current breath pattern. Count the length of your inhale, exhale, and the pauses in between. Do that for about thirty seconds.

- If you're not doing it already, begin to breathe through your nose.

- If the length of your exhale is the same as your inhale, just increase the length of your exhale so it's about two counts longer than your inhale. Allow the breath to move slowly and silently through you. No sharp inhales.

- After the exhale, pause for a second before inhaling. Try that a few times till it feels natural.

- Sense your face. Allow your eyes to soften, like in the soft eyes exercise in Chapter 5.

- Allow the outside corners of your lips to move slightly outward, in a tiny smile. Don't force it.

- As you exhale, think about allowing your bones to soften, your tension to melt, as if each breath were entering your bones.

- You may find as you practice this that your head wants to tilt a little to one side. This is perfectly natural. Allowing the neck to relax a little so that the head tilts as you breathe has been called the attitude of tender regard. This attitude is built into the human repertoire and is connected to the act of listening, entailing literally lifting an ear to connect with the other. Dog owners know this attitude, having experienced their dog looking at them with one ear cocked, ready to do their bidding.

When you breathe, gently smile, and soften your posture during an interaction, you literally can change how you listen, enabling others to do the same. We all respond to our environment and take our cues from a person's breath and expression, even if we are not consciously aware of it. Someone panicking on a plane or in a theater can cause chaos. By engaging in the breath and attitude of tenderness, you not only tone down your critical self, you also help others move out of judgment and into a place of listening.

CHAPTER 9

The Healer's Kryptonite – Attachment

Time heals all wounds, unless you pick at them.

—Shaun Alexander

There is a Native American saying that disease begins in the spirit, then moves to the emotions, and then finally manifests in the physical. Whether that's true or not, investigating your relationship to your wounds is essential in order to heal. No one consciously sits around and says, "I would like to be in pain."

When I was in college, I woke up one morning to a locked jaw. It hurt to open it more than about an inch. I couldn't bite an apple or even a hard-boiled egg. The doctor told me it was stress, which I couldn't believe or understand. I was having a wonderful time feeling freedom from my oppressive upbringing, finding my way as an adult. How could this be stress? He prescribed Valium, which just made me pass out. I didn't understand how to use it, so I threw it away. I became very good at talking while barely moving my mouth, and finding other ways to eat.

At that point in my life, I prided myself on being kind of a "tough chick." There had been a seminal moment four years before, when my father had started slapping me and I had refused to move or cry. I had simply stood there, enduring his rage, glaring at him. He never hit me again, and I hadn't cried since.

About a year and a half into my TMJD (Tempomandibular joint dysfunction) I found myself speaking to a nurse who was visiting a friend of mine. We were chatting, and somehow we got into talking about my childhood. I laughingly talked about my mother telling me never to trust anyone. That I should never let my guard down. That I should always be ready to protect myself. I proudly continued, talking about how that was why I broke up with guys before they could break up with me. That was why I made sure not to get too close to my friends and never to let anyone know that I was hurt.

All of a sudden, there was an explosion inside of me, and I started crying, sobbing uncontrollably, as if someone had pulled a switch and turned me into a puddle of grief. This poor woman who had never met me before simply sat there compassionately listening, the perfect teacher. I finally calmed down, apologized, and laughed in my embarrassment. Then I realized: my jaw had completely unlocked.

I had been holding old patterns from my childhood that were not congruent with who I wanted to be. Often, wounds are formed within us that we don't even realize, and then they begin to prevent us from becoming who we are. My TMJD was what Moshe Feldenkrais would have called an "anxiety pattern." I didn't know I was either anxious, or angry, or sad. Everything had gone into my jaw to protect my determination to be invulnerable. My emotional pain had become a physical pain. I was fortunate to have a breakthrough, but sometimes these attachments seem to literally eat us alive without us even realizing them, like parasites. I call them emotional gremlins; they're like invisible imps attached to different parts of us, feeding off our emotions, for our entire lives.

The Pain Body

"Pain is inevitable, suffering is optional." - Haruki Murakami,
What I Talk About When I Talk About Running

Like King Amfortas, the real wound may be unspoken, but the suffering manifests in how we navigate our lives.

What Is Pain?

The biological definition of pain is "an unpleasant sensory and emotional experience associated with actual or potential tissue damage or described in terms of such damage." One definition I read long ago was that the experience of pain is resistance to that sensation. At first this doesn't seem to make sense—what does it mean to resist a sensation? When you feel pain because of an injury, you are responding to a sensation at that spot. Certain nerve cells, called nociceptors, (*nocere* is the Latin word for harm) respond to threat or damage. Your brain calls it pain—it's designed to get your attention. In his book *A Guide to Better Movement* Todd Hargrove writes, "Sensation is the detection of a stimulus and the transmission of a signal to the nervous system." In other words, you touch a stove, you experience heat. You stand outside in winter; the sensation is cold. Perception, however, is the process of taking that sensory information, filtering it, organizing it, and interpreting its meaning to create a subjective or conscious experience related to sensation: this is unpleasant. You touch the stove, it's hot, the brain turns it into "ouch!" You step outside, the wind howls, you "resist the sensation" by shivering, hunching, and eventually getting a jacket. You cut yourself, the sensation is sharpness, the perception tells you that you need a band aid. This perception of pain is important. People who don't experience pain don't live very long, because they are unable to perceive that something is wrong and go without treatment until it's too late.

For many people, pain doesn't go away, even after an injury has healed. There are many reasons for chronic pain. Damage to the brain/nervous system pathway through injury, stroke, or other trauma can set up a loop that is difficult or even impossible to break. Sometimes after a trauma, fear of pain sets up a different kind of pain loop. Remember, the definition says: "described in terms of such damage." Emotional trauma often creates protective physical habits that result in various pain syndromes (like my TMJD.) Your attitude toward your pain can also affect the level of pain you experience. That's where suffering comes in.

One of the archaic definitions of suffering is "to allow." Perhaps the most famous use of the word in this context comes from the New Testament where Jesus admonishes the adults and says, "Suffer little children, and forbid them not, to come unto me . . . ," meaning allow them to approach. We allow suffering or As Murakami said in above quote, suffering is optional. It often doesn't *feel* like a choice. Who would choose suffering? Yet once the brain has created that loop, it can be difficult to untangle the connections and find new pathways.

Whether the holding is a protective habit, a fear response, or unconscious tension, it can sometimes create structural challenges that result in pain in a completely different part of the self.

Dr. John Sarno, who wrote the groundbreaking book *Healing Back Pain* as well as several others, dedicated his life to helping people relieve their pain. He called this unconscious holding TMS: tension myositis syndrome or tension myoneural syndrome. Some therapists equate this with MPS—myofascial pain syndrome. Whatever you call it, it is the result of different kinds of tension that impacts the movement and breath of your tissue.

Your cells breathe—cellular respiration is how your cells take oxygen and turn it into energy. Unconscious excessive tension literally deprives those tense parts of oxygen. That sensation then sends a signal to the brain, which translates as pain. This kind of wound to yourself can be the result of emotional and physical trauma, which may have begun as an unconscious protective mechanism but has now become a parasitic gremlin. Why do we hold on to these different wounds? The kryptonite of the healer is attachment: attachment to the wound, the pain, the fear of pain, the story of the pain.

There are two related terms that I have found very useful in looking at the healer's kryptonite. Woundology is a word that was created by Caroline Myss, a noted teacher and author of many books, including *Why People Don't Heal and How They Can*. According to Myss, Woundology is the tendency to insistently hold on to old traumas and to define yourself by your hurts, not your strengths. You can stay stuck forever in those hurts. Moshe Feldenkrais said, "We act in accordance with our self-image." A person who's invested in woundology has a wounded self-image. They introduce themselves as wounded. The first thing they talk about are their wounds. Their wounds have become their emotional gremlin. Every time you repeat your story about your wounds, you continue to feel and experience those wounds.

Catastrophizing is another word. It's sometimes also called cognitive distortion—literally seeing the worst possible place, the worst-case scenario, the dark side. "Oh, it's happening to me. I know that I have this. I know this is going to go badly. I know that this back pain that I have is actually going to require surgery." You can catastrophize about anything, not just physical issues: your boss looks at you strangely, and you go into paroxysms of anxiety that he wants to fire you; your date is late, and you are sure they have dumped you. Anxiety and fear create tension, triggering the sympathetic nervous system to shoot chemicals that cause knots and spasms, building up lactic acid in parts of the body contributing to both physical and emotional pain. It's hard to believe that the body would want to make this a habit, but with repeated triggers, you can actually become addicted to catastrophizing, your nervous system craving the chemicals that make you feel bad.

We develop these "parasitic" habits at certain points in our lives in order to survive, in order to get through something (like my familial contradictions leading to TMJD). These habits serve us for a certain amount of time, maybe for protection, or compensation for an injury, or simply to keep us from screaming out loud. Then they begin to steal our vitality by becoming invisible patterns. We don't even know they are there because we are so used to them. These emotional gremlins gleefully eat away at our potential joy.

The Payoff

When your self-image is attached to your wounds, it can be difficult to imagine a different life. "Working around" the injury, illness, pain, or sorrow becomes so habitual, any other life becomes impossible. The plasticity of the brain can work against you when you successfully adapt to living in woundology and catastrophizing. What would happen if you were no longer exhausted? There is a popular meme that people share that says, "I identify as tired," as if that is a badge of courage or a cross to bear. But if your illness or pain went away tomorrow, what would your life be like? Many people don't realize that by organizing themselves around their pain, they have created a strange kind of comfort. The nervous system doesn't discriminate about habits. It assumes that the repeated behavior is important for survival. It wants to hold on to the familiar, even if it sucks.

*"A man will renounce any pleasures you like but he
will not give up his suffering."* – **G.I. Gurdjieff**

Sometimes, there's an unconscious payoff to suffering. Your attachment to your wound could be keeping you from doing something else with your life. I sometimes ask my chronic pain clients, "What would happen if you were cured?" One hesitated, then said, "I'd lose my disability payments. I'd have to go back to work." Another said, "Are you kidding? I'd be ecstatic!" Then, after a pause, "I'd . . . I'd, be giving up my pain meds. And, I probably wouldn't need those naps in the afternoon . . ."

When you define yourself by your injury or pain, what would you have to talk about if it went away? It may sound crazy, but attachment to this injury, this wounded self-image, this story about your pain can be part of what keeps you in pain.

Where Are You Holding?

Close your hands into fists, and hold them tightly. Notice what you sense. There might be a sensation of heat or simply tightness. But eventually the sensation will come to a point of discomfort and pain. Let go and sense your hands. They're probably grateful that you let go! Energy and oxygen can return into your hands. They may also ache for minute. Letting go can initially seem painful!

Letting go seems like a no-brainer when you do something like this intentionally. But where are the other holdings, the wounds that you don't acknowledge? Those are the ones that activate the healer's kryptonite when you think of healing yourself.

*Nothing is permanent about our behavior patterns,
except our belief that they are so."* – **Moshe Feldenkrais**

Maybe you know your holding places: the gut, your shoulders, maybe even your toes. Perhaps there are hidden places that are currently unavailable to you. There is a popular "relaxation" technique where people tense and relax every part of themselves, starting with the feet and moving upward all the way to the face, part by part. This is a wonderful exercise and can help relax you. The muscles you intentionally tense and relax work in pairs called agonist and antagonist. When you tense a muscle, its partner needs to let go. This creates a relaxation response. However, in order to actually change a holding pattern, you need to add attention and intention. There is a different quality to clenching and unclenching your fists because you feel like you're going to explode and you do this mechanically versus making an intentional decision to pay attention to your hands in a moment of crisis. Attention: to yourself, to the sensation in the hands, to your holding patterns, can shift your attitude from one of holding and tension to healing and relief. The healer's center of presence, the power of the hands, then provides a talisman or an anchor in your healing process.

Paying Attention With Your Hands

Remember in Chapter 4 how there was a different sensation when you touched your forehead with your palm versus the back of your hand? Your face and your hand each felt something, even though you didn't necessarily have any kind of an emotional attitude when you touched the face. It was simply a sensation. Your brain fires in myriad places depending on the touch, the quality of the touch, and the repetition of the touch. When you add intention: to slap or caress, for example, you experience different sensations that trigger emotional reactions. When you add attention to intention, you are harnessing the energy in your hands.

- Touch your face. What is the sensation?

- Sit quietly and sense your breathing. Return your attention to your hands.

- Imagine you can feel the nerve endings, your meridian endings, the sensory process that goes from your hands to your brain. It doesn't matter if you don't know anatomy or don't believe in energy or meridians. You are just using imagery to bring more attention to a part of yourself.

- Now imagine the quality of love, compassion, or caring. There are many ways to picture this: with your action, your thought, and your feeling.

- Begin with your breath. You don't have to change anything or breathe in a particular way. Just attending to the breath with the *intention* of compassion can bring about a different emotional experience. If you wish, you can repeat the breath pattern of tender regard detailed in Chapter 8.

- Imagine someone you care for very much. See them in your mind's eye. It could even be a beloved pet. You can also simply allow the radiance of the idea of love to surround you. You may not suddenly feel overwhelmed with love, but it will be a different state than you were in when I simply asked you to touch your face without thinking a minute ago. Stay with the breath, the image, the feeling, and once again, touch your face. Notice what you feel. Then remove your hand from your face.

- Think for a moment, is there a place in you that has pain or sorrow, grief, anger, a wound? Stay with this feeling of compassion and touch that part of you. Just touch without trying to change or fix anything. The power of your hand and the power of your intention can begin to bring a healing energy into that spot. Of course, most of us have more than one such spot, but start small. Give yourself time to experience them one at a time.

- You can try this with others. Stand behind a friend, and place your hand on their shoulder in a quick, casual fashion. Remove your hand, tell them you are going to do it again. Before you do it, however, pause and close your eyes. Sense your breath. Imagine that you have all the love in the world for this person. Imagine that that love will be reflected in the way you touch their shoulder. Don't tell your friend what you are trying. Then place your hand on that person's shoulder. Ask them if the two contacts felt different.

Going Deeper

What are you holding on to?

What would happen if you let go of it?

What is the payoff for keeping your wound?

An Act of Self-Compassion

Suffering can sometimes twist into anger and bitterness; resenting the situation and punishing your body, literally "raging against the machine." This will only lead to more frustration and pain. Even anger can become habitual, creating an apparently endless cycle of suffering. Your emotions affect your chemistry, and your chemistry affects your emotions. It sounds crazy, but the nervous system becomes "attached" to this painful cycle.

Often when I work with someone who has chronic pain, at the end of the lesson, they sit up and the pain is gone. They start twisting and shifting and stretching, "looking" for their pain instead of appreciating the sensation of being pain free. The attachment to the habit of pain is so strong, they feel lost. Sometimes it takes repeated sessions for a person to be willing to say goodbye to this toxic companion!

By choosing instead to move slowly, gently, with intention and attention, you can begin to unravel the pain loop. Remember the pulsing motion from Chapter Four? When you take the time to attend to yourself by softly pulsing your hand, you can change your state from one of frustration or anger to an inner quiet. As you pulse your hand, move your hand to the pain spots you identified. The pulsing action of the fingers helps shine the light of attention on the places that need healing. This act of self-compassion becomes a loop of love that goes from brain to hand, from hand to body part.

Whether you choose to simply touch your wound with your loving hand or pulse it and hover above it, take the time to listen to yourself: your sensations, perceptions, thoughts and feelings. This is the path to healing.

Going Deeper

What would it take to shift your anger at your situation?

Why are you hard on yourself? Where did you learn that?

What would it take to have compassion for yourself?

CHAPTER 10

The Visionary's Kryptonite – Limitation

"Without learning to know ourselves as intimately as we possibly can, we limit our choice. Life is not very sweet without freedom of choice. Change is very difficult with no alternatives in sight. We then resign ourselves to not dealing with our difficulties as if they were prescribed by heaven."

— Moshe Feldenkrais

I stood in the park and marveled at the perfect organization of the hill. In my mind, I saw clearly that this hill, gently sloping down to a flat space, was like a natural amphitheater. I saw it all: crowds of people sitting on the hill, enjoying a variety of entertainments. I would be an impresario. I managed to score an outdoor stage from a traveling company, booked all my friends and colleagues for a summer of performances, and emptied my bank account to rent lights and sound equipment. I bragged about my vision: How I couldn't believe no one had ever seen the potential of this space. How this was going to change the culture of avant-garde theater in New Jersey (avant-garde theater in New Jersey? What was I thinking?).

And then . . . it rained. The first weekend, it poured all day, so we postponed the performance to the next weekend. Even though they predicted rain again, I insisted we try. We put up the lights. The performers got ready. The audience was small. After all, the grass was still wet from the rain the day before, and the clouds were lowering. The show began. And so did the rain. Before we even had a chance to begin covering the lights, the deluge began.

It rained every Saturday for the entire month. I don't know what was more painful—paying performers for shows they hadn't done, tearing up the stage because the parks department wanted it removed (oh such a lack of vision they had!) or admitting that in my visionary zeal, I had forgotten about the weather. I look back on it now, and admit that deep inside, I was still trying to desperately prove that I was not a failure, and so was literally blinded to circumstance.

Tunnel vision, lack of clarity, narrow perspective are all ways the visionary limits choice. Deep inside, my "vision" of myself was congruent with my father's perception that I was destined to be a failure. This desire to prove him wrong had limited my ability to see the "whole picture."

It took many more years to change my self-image and learn that making mistakes doesn't make you a failure, as long as you learn something new each time. Learning to "see" myself required removing the cobwebs from my brain: negative self-talk, fear of reprisal, the need for approval, and so much more. I still often feel the siren's call to embark on a fool's errand, some quixotic quest. But there is a bit less baggage on the journey, and my vision is a bit clearer as I navigate through my mistakes.

Blind Spots

"Every man takes the limits of his own field of vision for the limits of the world." — Arthur Schopenhauer

The visionary limits possibility by using perception to *not* see the whole picture. I refused to see the whole picture of producing a theater series because I was blinded by my "need to succeed." But another way of being blinded is by limiting possibility. It is much more difficult to see your perceived limitations, the inner voices that say, "You can't do that."

The word "perception" comes from percipere, the Latin word meaning "to seize, to understand." Its root words, *per-* "entirely" + *capere* "take," tell us that to perceive invites us to see the whole picture, not just a part.

Perceive

1. become aware or conscious of (something); come to realize or understand.

   "his mouth fell open as he perceived the truth"

   Similar:

   > become aware of (something) by the use of one of the senses, especially that of sight.

   > "he perceived the faintest of flushes creeping up her neck"

   Similar:

2. interpret or look on (someone or something) in a particular way; regard as.

"If Guy does not **perceive** himself **as** disabled, nobody else should"

We spoke earlier about the relationship of sensation and perception. But perception is also how you feel about yourself. Whenever you say to someone, "Oh, I could never do that," "I'm just not talented," or "Maybe in my next life," you are interpreting, looking on your life experience through the lens of limitation. It's interesting that the dictionary definition uses the sentence example "if Guy does not **perceive** himself as disabled, nobody else should" perfectly illustrating others' perception of Guy's limitations in contrast with his own perception of himself as *not* limited.

The first definition: "become aware or conscious of (something); come to realize or understand," contains within it the invitation to go beyond our ordinary perception and see something new. How can you see what you don't see? If you can't see what's limiting you, how can you begin to move past that particular limitation?

This image is likely familiar to you, a classic of perception and vision.

Some people immediately see a vase, others zero in on the two profiles. Some people have difficulty seeing the second image, some can switch back and forth. Can you see both at the same time? You can expand your vision so that you're not perceiving just one idea, just one possibility.

This is your brain at work. Your eyes take in the light, the rods and cones in your retina sort out the color and shape. The two hemispheres of your brain need to work together to say "vase" or "two profiles." If you have a focused tunnel vision on one thing, you're not necessarily able to take in everything that's happening. Your brain literally makes things disappear, organizing your universe. Your perception is the result: whether it's life situations, or how you see yourself. Many times we focus on just one thing about ourselves, and we can't see the other possibilities. Or we can't see what is limiting us because we're so focused on this one thing: "I'm not good enough." "I had a terrible childhood." "I have bad knees."

One of the dictionary definitions of limitation, "a condition of limited ability; a defect or failing," gives the following example: "she knew her limitations better than she knew her worth."

Our perceived limitations are so pervasive, even the dictionary illustrates how we limit ourselves! These limitations keep us from realizing our vision for ourselves. There are limitations, of course, in everyone. I would make headline news if I became a pro basketball player because I'm only five feet, two inches tall. (I actually did pass my basketball exam in college, but I think it was because the coach wanted to be sure she'd never see me again.) However, there are countless examples of people realizing their dreams in spite of life's challenges. The Paralympics are a classic example of people going beyond perceived limitations. Recently there was a TV series called The Queen's Gambit, which followed the life of a young woman in the 1960s becoming a world chess champion in spite of overwhelming obstacles. The series literally inspired millions to go learn to play chess. We celebrate those who see possibility where others see limitation.

What do you see? You can expand your vision in order to be able to see more possibility and be able to do what you want to do. You can develop an insight into yourself, so that you can create the vision for who it is you want to be.

When I was a young performer, I would write these passionately dramatic mime pieces. But when I performed them, instead of eliciting gut-wrenching empathy from the audience, they generated laughs. People laughed uproariously. No matter how hard I tried to make them see the pathos in my pieces, they found me funny. Distressed, I asked a mentor what I should do. He shrugged and said, "You need to learn to turn your liabilities into assets. Not everyone can make people laugh. Use the laughter to touch people."

Once you see that your limitations could become your strengths, you can turn them into something that's actually going to support you instead of just trying to overcome them. The father of hypnotherapy, Milton Erickson, was paralyzed by polio as a youth. While lying paralyzed in bed, unable to speak, he learned how to observe and listen. This ability became his strength. He once said, "Allow yourself to see what you don't allow yourself to see."

Each time you accept a limitation, your world becomes smaller. "I can't", "I don't," "not anymore," are phrases that stop us. Take a moment ask yourself, *What do I want for myself?* Is there something you want to do for yourself that has not been available to you thus far or that you seem to think is impossible? It doesn't have to be winning an Academy Award. It can seem inconsequential to others, for example, to be able to climb stairs or create a garden on your balcony.

- Close your eyes and envision it. What do you wish for yourself? Even if the answer is "I want to know what I want," write it down.

- How can you know what you don't know? How can you see what you don't see? Can you change your perception? Sit quietly for a moment and ask yourself, "How do I limit myself?" Whatever thoughts come up, jot them down.

Don't judge, and don't edit. Simply put words on the paper. And if no words appear in your mind, write down that there are no words . . . yet.

I was working with a client who had neck pain. He was lying on his side, and I gently took hold of his arm. "You remember that I came in here about my neck, not my arm, right?" he asked apprehensively. "Your neck is connected to your arm." "It is?" His eyes widened.

I discovered as I moved his arm, that there was very little range. As I lengthened the arm, then moved it toward the back, it would abruptly stop, as if the arm had slammed into a wall. "Am I hurting you?" I asked. "Huh? No." he replied. "Why did your arm stop?" I gently moved it forward and backward again. "It doesn't go any further," he said. I put down his arm and began to investigate the relationship between the shoulders, ribs, and head in various directions, always taking care to keep the head together with the shoulders and chest. I went back to his arm to move it forward and back, and suddenly, the arm moved much further, and he began to roll his head. "What the . . ." he sputtered. "I didn't even know I was tight back there!" He stood up, and his neck pain was gone. Beneficial side effect: his arms had gotten "longer."

"I guess it wasn't a neck problem," he shrugged.

Part of this process is to acknowledge that your obstacles are sometimes invisible. You've just been stopped. Don't keep banging on the same door.

Looking for Yes

As you look at your stated goal, what do you say no to? What is it that you're saying, "No, I can't do this" to? Maybe there are several different aspects to the thing that you say no to. "No, I don't like to go outside." "No, people will hate my work." "No, I will be rejected by my daughter or my husband." How do you say no to yourself? Look inside yourself for a moment, think of that no, and ask yourself where you feel the no. Do you feel it in your chest, in your breath, in your belly, in your fists? Where is the sensation of refusal? Don't dwell on it, simply identify it.

We used to play different games wherein objects were hidden, whether it was an Easter Egg or a scavenger hunt. You would search, looking everywhere and not finding anything—then suddenly, aha! When you reveal your "no," it's like discovering the secret prize under the rock. It was there all along; you just needed to know how to look. Once you find the "no," it's the first step to "yes."

Seeing Inside

In order to see inside yourself, you need to stop looking outside. The following exploration is done with eyes closed. So even though the entire sequence is written below, you need a different strategy to actually do it (unless you can read with your eyes closed!). Option 1: you can read this entire section, then play with the ideas with your own timing. Option 2 (recommended): click on the QR Code – audio for a more comprehensive version and enjoy.

While your intention is to make this an exploration of looking within, it will also affect your outer vision. Look at something in your room; how do you focus in on it? Take a moment to see *how* you see right now. Be curious. Make sure the room temperature is right. If you wear glasses, take them off. Make yourself comfortable. If you're uncomfortable lying down, you can this do sitting up, although it's more relaxing to do it lying down.

- Lie on your back. You can have your legs elongated, bent, or on a pillow or bolster. For the purposes of this lesson, during the rests, feel free to switch to lying on your side or any other comfortable position. Just remember to keep your eyes closed throughout the exercise.

- Tune into your contact with the floor, the quality of your breath.

- Turn your attention to your face. Notice the muscles in the cheeks. Imagine the two sides of your face just sinking toward your ears on each side, as if they could yield to gravity. Allow your mouth to relax. If you're sitting, just make sure that your mouth is soft.

- Sense your eyes resting in your head, their size and shape. Allow your attention to travel around the orbits of your skull as if tracing a circle. The eyes really much larger than we think they are, about the size of apricots. They go back into the skull, so big that the bottom of the eyes is just a fraction of an inch above the roof of your mouth.

- Allow your eyes to sink into the skull. You can imagine that behind your eye there are little satin pillows, and you're just letting the eyes rest on those pillows. You don't need any effort right now in your eyes.

- Sense your eyelids. Is there any tension in your eyelids right now?

- This is more imagination than reality: allow your eyelids to press your eyeballs downward into those pillows and then release several times. You've already begun exploring possibility and impossibility! Who would think that your eyelids could press your eyes into your head and release? Just play. Don't worry if it doesn't feel possible. Let that go, and just sense the eyeballs again.

- Raise your right hand and place the heel of your palm on your right cheekbone. Cup your palm around your eye with the fingers pointing toward the middle of your forehead. Don't press on the eyeball. Then take the left hand and cup the left eye in the same way so that your hands cross across the bridge of your nose. Keep your elbows soft so that everything is relaxed. You don't have to tense any part. Your eyes are closed, your hands are cupped, so that you're looking into a field of blackness. You don't have to stare. You can just allow the blackness to come into your eyes.

- Imagine that as you're breathing, the blackness is like a pulse that flows with the inhale and exhale across your field of vision. Notice whether it feels completely black or whether you're seeing little sparks of color or areas that seem lighter or darker.

- Leaving your eyes closed, bring your arms back down. Sense how the light wants to filter through your eyelids now.

- Turn your attention to your right eye. Begin moving your right eye to the right, as if you wanted to look at your right ear, and then return to the center. Of course, your left eye will participate, but keep your attention on the right eye. As you move your eye, do you feel anything in the back of your head? In your neck? You might even sense your shoulder on the right side a little bit differently. What happens if you let your eye move to the right as you pay attention to the experience of sensing your right side? Notice your breath. Do you sense your right hip? the right side of your waist? Your jaw? As your eye is moving to the right, it can look inwards toward all those places.

- Pause a moment and rest.

- Resume attending to your right eye, this time moving it to the left, toward the bridge of your nose. Can you still pay attention to your right side? It's as if your eye is now moving away from your right shoulder. Can you feel that in your belly? In your jaw? In the roof of your mouth?

- Rest.

- Compare the sensation of your right eye and your right side to the left.

- Turn your attention to your left eye. Just notice, does the left eye itself feel different as it sits in your skull?

- Begin this same exploration, moving your left eye to the left. First follow just the path of the movement. How does this eye travel? What do you pay attention to? What can you see? If you give your attention to one eye, can you still sense the other?

- Allow your attention to travel through your left side. Notice each time you look to the left how you can connect with another part of yourself, maybe all the way down to your left pinky toe.

- What do you feel in your tongue? In the side of your neck? Then pause again. Try moving your left eye to the right while you continue to attend to your left side, going inward and downwards toward your belly.

- Rest.

- Once again, place your hands on your eyes the way you did in the beginning, and look into the field of blackness. Your hands are on your face, just looking into the blackness. Notice if the blackness has changed in any way for you after doing that. Notice the blackest area. For me, it's always in a corner, but maybe you have it in the middle. Imagine that that black area is like an ink spill. Let that ink spread across the field of your vision so that the whole field of your vision becomes a liquid pool of black.

- Remove your hands and rest.

- Imagine a thread that goes from your right eye to your right big toe, like a fishing line or a filament that travels right from your eye and connects up to your right big toe. Try to see that line with your mind's eye.

- Imagine a little pearl or a little bead strung onto the line. You don't actually have to see a pearl, just imagine it's there.

- With your eye, begin to watch that imaginary pearl move from the center of your eye all the way down to your big toe, along that line. As you're seeing that line of yourself, your vision traveling down to your big toe, and then traveling back up all the way to your eye, imagine that as you're making this trip, you're also sensing the parts of yourself underneath the pearl. As the pearl travels along this string, sense your neck, your ribs, your pelvis, the top of your leg, all the way down to your toes, the whole right side of yourself.

• Repeat this a few times, pausing at points along the way to sense yourself, noticing if you hit blank spots.

• Finding places that seem invisible is incredibly useful, because it means your brain map doesn't have enough information about that region—either due to lack of use, unawareness, or even old injury. They are blind spots in your sensory self-image. Notice where you want to stop, where you want to resume. As you move the pearl up and down, what do you sense as you travel through those thick places, those dark places in yourself? Can you see what you don't usually see? Take the time to pause where you need to illuminate something.

• Just a few times, take that pearl and zip it as if it's on a zip line, zooming down to your big toe and then back up to your eye, five times as fast as possible.

• Rest and sense the difference between your right side and your left side, your right eye and your left eye.

• Try the same thing with your left eye.

• You don't have to be good at this. No one will ever know. You don't have to succeed. After all, there's really no line there. You're just imagining or pretending that it's there. It's all in your head, as they say. There are many ways to shine the light of attention on ourselves.

• Once again, bring your hands over your eyes as you did before, and look into your field of blackness. Let your eyes rest in lush black velvet. Then take your hands away. Recall what you wrote before you began this journey. Return your attention to that place in yourself that said "no" or to that sensation of impossibility. Can you bring your eyes to softly look down into that area? Maybe it's an injury. Maybe it's an emotion. Maybe it's just a ball of tension that lives inside a part of you. Can you allow your eyes to softly gaze? Not stare, not pinpoint, but simply allow your inner vision to illuminate your holding place? Imagine a ball of light expanding from that area of challenge. Maybe you have a few places that you want to explore in this way. Then let that go.

- Very slowly open your eyes a tiny bit, as if you were looking through your eyelashes, just beginning to let light start to come in. Gradually open your eyes and just take in what's around you right now. Can you look outward while still having a sensation of yourself in contact with the floor, your breath, your emotional state? How do you see yourself now? G.I Gurdjieff often stressed the importance of the ability to be able to "see myself as I am."

- Slowly come up.

How do you take in your room now?

Going Deeper

How do you see yourself?

Can you draw a picture of your illuminated self?

What is your relationship with your personal obstacles now?

How can you open your vision to your possibilities instead of limitations?

There is research that explores the relationship of the movement of the eyes to the right and the left, and how that movement of the eyes connects up to your viscera, your muscles, your tensions, even the hemispheres of the brain.[xv] Attentively moving the eyes can help you recognize sensations connected with perceived limitations or challenges. Noticing how your eyes move and where they jump or feel awkward can offer clues about your perceptions.

Because of the way the brain and nervous system map themselves, your eyes offer feedback about your self-image.

Maria is a working actress with a wonderful stage presence. Her characters are fully realized; she embodies whatever she is playing. Yet off stage, she has struggled with anxiety and a perceived sense that people are "out to get her." Whether it's a hidden trauma, or a pattern she grew up with, Maria seems to always suffer physical challenges like muscle spasms and a stiff neck, as well as unexplainable fatigue. I noticed that she had a habit of bulging her eyes out at random times, looking like a deer in headlights. She was not only wide-eyed, but her eyes often trembled, jumping rapidly, displaying what is called nystagmus. When we are shocked or frightened, our eyes "jump" forward as if we are trying to see everything around, including a potential escape. A person frozen in terror feels trapped, the eyes bulging, darting, hyper-vigilant. Maria had never connected her symptoms with the use of her eyes. While she still struggles with a sense of anticipatory dread, she now recognizes her eyes' "fear pattern" and has been able to use eye movements to both calm her anxiety and relieve her physical tension.

You don't have to live in a place of limitation. Simply look at what says, "No." Is it real, or is it just a perception? There is no point in trying to push past your perceived limitation, because the limitation itself will stop you. But you can go *toward* it. The first step is to see. What's behind the curtain? Is it the great and powerful NO? Or is it simply another gremlin desperately trying to distract from seeing YES, pulling levers and shouting to distract you?

Whether it's physical, mental, or emotional, once you unveil your perception, the experience of limitation changes. Each time you look at yourself, you will discover something. In that process, the limitation itself will shift, and new possibilities will emerge.

PART III

Your Archetypal Superpowers

I once heard a radio program where people were asked what superpower they would choose: either the ability to fly, or to be invisible. But if we all had that ability, would it be a superpower? Or is it what you do with the superpower that changes the equation?

Each of us has abilities that if cultivated, will allow us to become the fully realized persons we dream about. It's not about being "born" with a talent or superpower, or conversely, feeling you have to "work hard" in order to get anywhere. Yes, practice is necessary to get into the Olympics or to write a best seller. By learning to access and develop your archetypal superpowers, the process of learning, practicing, improving, and succeeding become a joy. And you will not only be able to achieve what you are aiming for, you will learn to be a shape shifter, able to adapt to any situation and benefit from every experience. That is a superpower beyond measure.

CHAPTER 11

The Warrior's Superpower: Intent

"Oh, you never know where you're going till you get there!"
— Sylvester the Cat

When I was about nine years old, my family went hiking at the local state park. We had gone there many times and explored many different trails. One day, my father led us down a new path. "Where are you taking us, Leo?" asked my mother, a little worried. "I don't know," shrugged Leo, "But the path has to be going somewhere." As we walked, the path led into a swamp. Strange plants and ominous bubbles in the muck inspired visions of goblins and quicksand. As the path got narrower and muddier, my mother started to cry. "We're lost! We'll never find our way out!"—words I'll never forget. They echo for me each time I feel I've lost my way, whether it's while I'm hiking or looking at the trajectory of my life. After the swamp, the path virtually disappeared, and we found ourselves bushwhacking through brambles, my sister and I trying desperately to not be as hysterical as our mother. (To this day, the memories of my mother's predilection for dire drama help slap me back to reality when I feel panicked.) A clearing appeared. We dashed for the opening and found ourselves in a parking lot. In the next town.

Joseph Campbell famously said that "As soon as you're sure you've found the path, you can be pretty sure it's not the path." How can you stay the course if the course keeps disappearing? How can you be sure you are going where you think you're going, or that you are doing what you think you're doing?

The warrior's superpower is the ability to follow through, to turn intention into action without getting waylaid along the path. That doesn't mean having tunnel vision, (one of the visionary's kryptonites). It's the ability to recognize options and obstacles without getting distracted from the aim.

Carlos Castaneda wrote a series of books about his adventures studying with a Yaqui Indian shaman named Don Juan. His aim was to become a "sorcerer." But in order to achieve his aim, Don Juan said Castaneda needed to first become a warrior and learn the art of "stalking." For thousands of years, humans practiced stalking in order to hunt for dinner. Today the most stalking you have to do for dinner is nail a parking spot at Trader Joes (ah that triumphant feeling!). Focus, attention to the environment, accuracy, and courage were essential to bring home the bacon. It's unfortunate that contemporary culture associates the concept of stalking with shady characters trolling the Internet or sexual predators. Don Juan wasn't talking about stalking dinner or other people. He taught the art of "stalking oneself." He emphasized that in order to have intent, the warrior's superpower, you need to stalk—or as we might put it today, attend to—what is taking place in yourself.

Intent, Intention, Attention

- Without overthinking it, write down some things that you want; your current intentions. It could be anything, from "I'd like to like myself more" or "I'd like to be able to pick up my grandchild" to "I want to create a financial empire." What are your intentions? Allow a quick, free association, jotting down the dreams that pop into your head right now.

- Look at what you have written and ask yourself, "What are the obstacles to realizing this intention?" What's blocking your path on your journey to your intent? Sometimes it's difficult, or even impossible, to see what's in your way. Sometimes the obstacle is simply your belief that attaining the goal is impossible because you see obstacles that are not really there.

Put the paper aside for now, and let's explore some of Don Juan's principles accessing the warrior's superpower.

Know Your Battleground

You have to see your situation clearly before you can actually begin to try to move toward your intention. This may seem to be obvious, yet we so often miss what's really taking place in front of us—whether by blinding ourselves or simply not attending to our deeper instincts.

At one point in my performing career, I had written a theater piece that needed financial backing. I met two producers who seemed perfect. Everything that they said was right. They found a great venue, seemed so cooperative and enthusiastic. At our contract meeting, I was thrilled that someone wanted to support my work. As soon I left the meeting, I got mysteriously, violently sick to my stomach for several hours.

It was only after they absconded with both the costumes and the profits that I realized I had not assessed the environment, had not attended to the signs around my "battleground." My body had been trying to warn me and I had ignored it.

Proprioception, exteroception (sensing the environment), and intero-ception create our sixth sense, the kinesthetic sense. To know your battle-ground means you are not only aware of your outer surroundings, but also of your experience of yourself in your surroundings. When you are discon-nected from these, you literally stumble through life. Everyone has had an experience like my story, where if only you had paid attention, you would have known this date you went on would be a disaster, or this new boss was going to be a problem, but instead, you didn't attend to the feeling in the pit of your stomach, or the tension in your shoulders, because . . . Lack of attention can appear on a simpler scale: you're walking across the room, and suddenly you stumble across a box. You're amazed: how did that box get there? Or you're looking for your glasses, and they're on top of your head. This lack of attention is what keeps you from actually realizing your intent.

Take a moment right now and sense yourself in your room. You know your room. You know that there are pictures behind you on the wall or that the couch is seven feet away. You have a clear sense of how you are in that space. How do you know that? How do you remember that? Close your eyes for a moment. See your space in your mind's eye, cataloguing the details. When you open your eyes and look around, notice what you missed. Even as you're looking around and determining that yes, it's all there, you will be surprised at what you miss, because sometimes things are so habitual, you no longer see them.

You can explore and develop this ability with your family or friends.

1. Go into a room together and assess the room. Then close your eyes, while the other person removes an item or moves something around in the room. Open your eyes and see if you can identify what's changed.

2. Close your eyes, and ask your friend to walk somewhere in the room. Count to five and ask them to stop. Can you sense where they are in the room? And if you are right or wrong, can you simultaneously sense how you feel inside? Triumphant? Frustrated? Bored? There is an oft repeated saying: *How you do one thing is how you do everything.* As you evolve your ability to sense and observe, you will find that your awareness of your inner "battleground" improves as well.

Discard What is Unnecessary

In order to realize their intent, warriors must make their actions congruent with their intention. As we know from the kryptonite chapters, it's easy to fall into self-sabotaging actions that actually interfere with the stated intention. What does it mean to discard everything that is not necessary? That extra trip to the fridge before you make that phone call. Turning on the TV when you said you wanted to write that article. Discarding everything that is not necessary requires an inner sincerity.

We don't always fill our lives with frivolous activities that distract us from our intent. I recently worked with Matthew, who had originally come to see me about chronic back pain. We both soon realized it was about so much more. A talented fitness trainer, he had been encouraged to create video courses illustrating the energy/motion connection. But he just couldn't get started; it seemed like "life" always got in the way. No matter how many clients he got, there was always another bill, always another responsibility that no one else could take care of. His mantra was, "I'd love to, but I don't have time."

When Covid hit, he suddenly had time—the gym shut down. He even had money, because he got unemployment. He dove into making the videos he had dreamed about. However, never having worked in the medium before, his work was amateurish, his presentation sloppy. He decided to share them on social media anyway. When the feedback was less than enthusiastic, he announced that he really hated social media and marketing. It never occurred to him to take a course or hire someone to help him.

The minute he was able to go back to his "day job," he dove back into busyness, abandoning his project. He would get back to his project soon, "when I have more time." He was unable to relax because he kept worrying about how he should be working on the videos. Then the back aches began, and it became excruciating to train people to be fit when he himself was in so much pain. As we worked together, he began to realize that his fear of failure in a new enterprise was literally "holding him back." Intimidated by the hugeness of his vision, he was unable to see how to begin to move from being a one-on-one trainer to a YouTube sensation.

However, sometimes discarding the unnecessary is not so obvious. Matthew started by observing and stopping his excuses, even though they were really good. He began to see that he had created a lot of unnecessary activity: scrolling through Facebook "as research" even though he said he hated it, helping out at the gym after hours because "someone's got to do it," even sitting around and worrying about his back pain and catastrophizing.

As he got clearer, Matthew realized that he didn't really want to become an online influencer. He had built this "dream" based on what others thought he should be doing. He realized that what made him happy was

121

working with individuals, helping one person at a time. Once he discarded the unnecessary idea of "you have so much talent, you ought to build an empire," his back pain went away. Sometimes discarding what's unnecessary means letting go of what you think you should be doing, and doing what you really want.

Take a Stand

It's one thing to say you want to create videos, it's another to actually do it. It also takes courage to acknowledge that you really *don't* want to do something. Taking a stand—whether it's becoming an activist and becoming a media darling, simply asking for what you want from your partner, or even accepting failure—is a courageous act. We are often exhorted to "feel the fear and do it anyway." In the previous warrior chapters, you learned certain ways to ground and center yourself. You can enhance this sense of power by learning to embody the emotion of courage. Yes, it is an emotion!

Throughout human history, people have attempted to codify the embodiment of emotions. Ancient Indian acting texts (who would think there were acting schools three thousand years ago?) list nine basic emotions or *rasas*. Courage is one of them. Scientists like Paul Eckman and Susanah Bloch each have identified six basic emotions, although they don't agree on which six.

Courage is not a basic emotion, but a complex mix. The list of complex emotions in most languages encompasses hundreds of words and levels of nuance. Courage in battle may look different than courage in asking for a raise. (Imagine Mel Gibson's character in *Braveheart* confronting a corporate boss, and you get the picture.) And yet, some of the same physiological factors can be involved; it's simply a question of level of intensity. When you need to "take a stand," you can support yourself by employing breath and posture strategies that can help you feel stronger and more able to stick to your intent.

In Chapter 2, I talked about the power pose and its possibilities and limitations. A colleague of mine did an experiment with a group of participants. The students all struck the pose, first facing away from others, and then facing each other. Some felt stronger, but many felt awkward and uncomfortable in a non-habitual pose. My colleague then had them lie down and explore some embodied movement sequences, similar to some of the lessons in this book. When the class attempted the pose again, most were able to sense a greater ability to inhabit the pose. While you can "fake it till you make it," finding an inner stability can help you more effectively take a stand. Going back to some of the movement explorations in both Chapter 2 and Chapter 6 can prepare you to stand up for yourself.

Breath of Courage

In order to embody courage, you don't have to look fierce or even powerful. You certainly don't have to strike a power pose. However, it's interesting to look at how simply playing with your breath and facial expression can influence your mindset. In  Chapter 3, you learned the "breath of impartiality" or neutral breathing. As you sit here, see if you can recall that breath, and if you can't, take a moment to go back and review it again. Remember, it's an inhale through the nose and exhale through the mouth, keeping both the inhale and exhale the same length and without pausing after either. It is quiet and relaxed, without pushing. It's always good to return to a neutral or zero place before exploring a different posture or emotional attitude so things don't get mixed up.

- Once you feel centered, simply change the pathway of the exhale. Instead of exhaling through the mouth, begin to exhale through the nose, which for many people feels natural. However, keep the inhale and exhale the *same length*, without pausing more than is needed to change from in to out and out to in. Allow the breath to move from the diaphragm; in other words, don't breathe by raising your shoulders or upper chest. Just try this breath for about fifteen breaths, then let it go.

- Sense your face. In Chapter 1, you had a chance to experience your face and habitual facial expression. You can return to Chapter 1 and review it. Staying with this sensation of your face, think of the muscles of your face moving outward, "abducting" away from your nose. The corners of the mouth move out while the corners of the eyes move toward your temples. You don't have to strain, although you may feel the invitation to smile, like you experienced in finding the tender regard of the teacher.

- Now let those muscles "adduct" coming in toward your nose. Don't worry about doing it well. Allow the lips to become a little thinner, not pursing as if you were going to kiss, but pressing toward each other. Keep your forehead smooth, but let your lower eyelids come in and up a little, as if you were focusing on something in the distance. Play with sensing the difference between abducting (smiling) and adducting (tightening/focusing.)

- Stand up. Put one foot in front of the other, as if you were about to take a step. This stance is actually a warrior stance. With one foot forward you are ready to move in any direction. In Asian martial arts, this stance is called *hanmi*. In fencing it's *en garde*. At a race, it's "on your mark." Begin to breathe through the nose, as described above—same length of inhale and exhale. Sense your center of presence, your pelvic region. Tighten your face a little bit, adducting the muscles. You will feel a little tension in your nose. You may feel inspired to tighten your hands into fists or put a little energy into your shoulders, as if someone was holding you back and you are pressing forward

- Then let it go; perhaps go back to your neutral breath or just shake out all over.

When you actually need to take a stand, you can try this breath and posture for a few minutes before your meeting. Or you can simply try it whenever you want to feel more energized and powerful. Make it your own. Create your own power process.

While this is a pattern that has been observed and studied, each of us has subjective relationships to the names we give to different feelings. Exploring an emotional pattern can feel artificial at first, like putting on the power pose from Chapter 2. There is no need to force yourself; instead, explore the elements you find interesting.

You can also create your own step into power. In the TV series *Ted Lasso*, there is a character named Rebecca, the CEO of the worst soccer team in England. In one episode she shares her process for building courage. "I make myself big!" she says (and she is not a small woman), and then demonstrates stretching herself in every direction, taking a deep breath and then roaring (remember the lion exercise in Chapter 2?!). It is comic, but at the same time illustrates the power of making an embodiment choice when you need to take a stand.

Going Deeper

As you look at the list of your intentions and the associated obstacles, can you clarify what you see as your battleground?

Where do you need to take a stand?

Can you give yourself permission to practice the embodiment of courage?

Relax

I often tell my students, "When the going gets tough, the tough lie down." Sometimes you need to just let go and allow things to happen. You've done all you can, and you don't know what to do next. Go lie down. It's not giving up. It's an intentional act. There's actually a movement brewing around the world called the lying flat movement. (Actually lying flat has been around since the time of Diogenes in ancient Greece.) Think of any hero's journey. There's a time when the hero has exhausted everything and needs to just sit under a tree. Often they have a dream that offers a solution. Or that is the moment they are visited by the mysterious dwarf, or wizened crone, who offers the next step. When you intentionally lie down, you are inviting new wisdom to come in. There is a Zen saying: You cannot fill a cup that is already full. Take a moment, empty yourself. Lie flat. Castaneda wrote that when you relax and abandon yourself, "Only then will the powers that guide us open the road and aid us."

Know When To Retreat

"Retreat, hell! We're not retreating, we're just advancing in a different direction." – Major General Oliver P. Smith, *Korean War's Battle of Chosin Reservoir*

. . . You've got to know when to hold 'em
Know when to fold 'em
Know when to walk away
And know when to run . . .

– Kenny Rogers "The Gambler"

Retreat does not mean surrender. It's taking time to regroup, recover, reconnoiter, reintegrate, and reverse. If you feel like you've gone to the point of no return, you have eliminated your options. Being able to reverse direction is wisdom, not cowardice. It means you survive to try again. The challenge is to *know* when to make this choice, and why you are doing it. It's not about retreating at the first obstacle. One of the warrior's superpowers is the ability to move in any direction. In the art of Aikido, there are many techniques of moving backward in order to allow the opponent to rush headlong right past you. Sometimes that means side stepping an obstacle, and sometimes it means to reverse. Reversibility is a key to functional action. When you get to the edge of the cliff, you want to know you have the option to back off, step away. You don't want your only option to be jumping like a movie action hero into the raging river below. Retreat gives you time to reexamine your options for a more effective strategy.

Choosing to Reverse

- Stand up and sense how your feet connect to the floor. If you can be barefoot, it's ideal. Allow yourself to sway a little forward and back, side to side, noticing how your feet and ankles adjust to the changes in direction. Don't go too far back!

- Sway forward enough that you have to take a step to catch yourself. How did that feel? Remember in Chapter 2, we talked about the power pose as only effective in certain situations. Standing with your feet on the same plane can throw you off balance. Instinctively, your foot knew to step forward so you didn't fall on your face.

- Remain with one foot in front of the other. Try the swaying again. You'll notice that you can't really sway with stiff legs.

- Change the sway to shifting your weight, slightly bending the front knee as you go forward and bending the back knee as you go backward. You have created the option for moving in either direction. You are once again in *hanmi*: the warrior stance. When you truly need to "step" into your power, you need that one foot forward so that you have the choice to move in any direction.

Some of you may remember Inigo Montoya's amazing swordfight in *Princess Bride*. If you go back and watch, you'll see that retreat is an essential part of that battle. *Hanmi* is a posture that prepares you to be able to have movement choices—you can step forward or back, as well as turn quickly. From this versatile place, simply shift your pelvis forward, to go over your front foot, then return over your back foot. Sensing how your pelvis can support you and connect to your legs brings vitality to your root *chakra*. Remember that the warrior's center of presence is the pelvis.

- As you shift back and forth, sense your *dantian*, the point of power below your belly button. Bring your attention to that power center as you move. Switch your legs and repeat.

- Then walk around your room, noticing the power flowing down your legs.

In a universe of endless possibilities, we often encounter surprises. Sometimes it's an injury or overwhelming odds due to finances or even corruption. Knowing when it's important to forge ahead and when it's wiser to back off requires sincerity with yourself. If I had been sincere with myself during my doomed production, I would have saved myself and my cast a lot of misery.

Going Deeper

Can you remember a time when you retreated from a situation? Take a moment to replay it for yourself. As you unfold the scene, notice your sensations, in the pit of your stomach, in your shoulders, in your breath. Think about how you felt after you backed off.

Were there other options?

How do you feel now?

Are You Doing What You Think You Are Doing?

In order to realize your intent, you need to make your actions congruent with your intentions. When you reach for a cup of coffee, it's pretty easy:

Desire, object of desire: coffee, command the arm, success. You don't even have to think about it, your intention and action are so clear. But perhaps you've had the experience of reaching for the cup of coffee just as your phone lit up with a text from your ex. Sometimes situations put us at cross purposes. Sometimes it's simply lack of attention. Have you ever started driving to run errands and suddenly found yourself at the exit to your office? (This of course, has *never* happened to me . . .) The relationship between intention and action makes the difference in whether or how you succeed. Whether it's in trying to accomplish an outer task, or changing a life habit, attending to your choices creates the result.

Even if you want to, you can't be trying to be a Zen master every moment of your day: Now, I am breathing, now I am chopping onions, now I am going to turn left. You'd never get out of your driveway. But you can develop functional habits that increase your ability to attend to your intention. One way to develop this skill is to practice exploring congruence when there is nothing at stake, like doing small meditative movements that clarify intent. As you try the following meditative movements, pay attention to where your mind goes. By practicing developing attention in this way, you will find yourself better able to apply attention and intention to your life choices.

Embodying Intent

- Find a place to lie down, on the floor or on your bed. If you want to do this with eyes closed, you can access a longer version of this sequence.

- Sense the parts of you in contact with the surface: how your back connects, the sensation of your arms and legs, your weight. This is your proprioceptive sense at work.

- Now extend your attention to include your relationship with the room, sensing the distance of your arms from either side of the room. How far is the wall from your right arm? How far is the wall from your left arm? Depending on where you are in the room, it's going to be a different experience. What do you feel above your head? Is there a sensation above your head? Can you feel the area above your head? How far can you feel the ceiling? Is there a sense of the ceiling? This is exteroception, sensing everything about the outside of yourself. From the standpoint of the warrior, you are sensing your "battleground."

- Return to the parts of you that connect to the floor or bed, and notice what *doesn't* connect to the floor.

- Notice your breathing and turn your attention to your *dantian*. Remember that the *dantian* is located about two and a half inches below your belly button right in the center of you, the core of yourself.

- Reconnect to your five cardinal lines from Chapter 1, but now, think of them emanating from this *dantian*. Notice their clarity, thickness, maybe even a color. This is the power of your interoceptive ability. To begin to know what you are doing, you have to know how you are.

- Expand the field of your attention to be able to see all five lines at the same time. Sense the movement of the *dantian* as you breathe, and then expand your attention outward again, sensing your room. You've got the general and the specific in multiple ways right now.

- Try to maintain a sense of your five lines as you bend one leg at a time and bring your feet so that they're flat on the floor, your knees facing the ceiling. How do you bend your legs? How many different ways can you bend your legs? Out to the side? Straight up? How slowly can you move?

- Go slowly enough that you can feel how your cardinal lines move as you move. When you lose something, pause and re-sense so that you really have clarity on what happens to your shape.

- As you bend and straighten your knees, what does your pelvis do? Does the *dantian* move? Explore this apparently simple act of bending and straightening your legs. Really pay attention. How do your legs influence your pelvis? How does your pelvis support your legs?

- Notice if you're doing anything extra. Tightening the shoulders, the lips, the jaw, or holding your breath. Discard everything that is unnecessary.

- Pause. Notice if anything has let go. Where do you still feel holding?

- Repeat the exploration of bending one leg at a time, but this time, turn your attention to your tension. When do you tighten, and when do you relax? It's amazing how much unnecessary tension we carry in ordinary activities, even silly ones, like bending the legs when nothing is at stake. There is no need to strive, to tense. Fear nothing.

- After exploring yourself in this way, take a moment to notice if you are still able to sense your five lines. Where did they go as you moved? Sense the *dantian*, the lines, yourself in the room, and see if you can stay connected to all of these different things as you come to stand and sense yourself in the room.

Taking Your Superpower into the World

The neuroendocrinology researcher Robert Sapolsky recently asserted that humans don't have free will, that everything we do is a mechanistic reaction based on our environment, culture, genetics, and fetal development.[xvi] We've got millions of years of history pushing us to simply be big-brained versions of Pavlov's dog. And yet . . . you *can* build intent and outwit Mother Nature. Harriet Tubman had absolutely no advantages in environment or culture. While it's true we can't trace her genetics, we can assert that she lived with intent and changed the lives of many as a result. Was it simply an oversupply of dopamine that drove her? Parsifal was raised by a single mother who hid him from anything that had to do with becoming a knight. What called him to pursue the Holy Grail? My parents firmly believed I was destined for disaster because I had not found a husband by age sixteen and did everything they could to dissuade me from a career in show business. Ironically, it was my dad who inspired me to keep going. He often repeated the saying, "Where there's a will, there's a way," when I was growing up. Maybe, according to Sapolsky, that developed my neurochemistry to prove them wrong. (Thank you, Dad!) If neuroplasticity (the brain's ability to change and adapt) is a fact, then you can use your experiences to develop the intent to be and do what you want with your life. It just takes practice.

One Small Step

You don't have to be a revolutionary to be the change you want to see in the world. Small acts of courage, like knocking on a neighbor's door to talk about their barking dog, asking for a raise, or wearing a sexy dress all require intent. If you start with something apparently small, you will find each successive act a little easier. Even if it's simply tackling your closet or joining a gym. Change one thing and you change everything.

"Whatever you can do or dream you can do, begin it.

Boldness has genius, power, and magic in it. Begin it now."

— William Hutchison Murray

CHAPTER 12

The Teacher's Superpower – Listening

True empathy is always free of any evaluative or diagnostic quality.

— Carl Rogers

It is said that the psychologist Carl Rogers often didn't say a word during his sessions but simply listened and that people felt transformed because of this. He said, "When people are listened to sensitively, they tend to listen to themselves with more care and to make clear exactly what they are feeling and thinking."[xvii]

Listening is not just hearing. The words we hear and the words we use when we speak are one layer of the content that is being communicated. In body language studies conducted over many years, it has been shown that the content of what is being said is a small percentage of what is being communicated. Back in the 1960s, Albert Mehrabian stated that only 7 percent of our communication is words.[xviii] However, he didn't even include body postures in his equation!

Still, words have power in them. As mentioned in Chapter 3, some of our most ancient cultures have myths about how the gods gave humans the gift of language. The Hebrew creation myth says, "In the beginning was the *WORD* . . ." How do words make your world?

When you listen to someone, you are listening to the words as well as taking in the speaker's attitude. At the same time, you can be listening to yourself. You can develop the ability to distinguish between sincerity and lies, between the slavery of habit and the freedom of choice in your intentions and actions.

> *"The word is not just a sound or a written symbol. The word is a force; it is the power you have to express and communicate, to think and thereby to create the events in your life. You can speak. What other animal on the planet can speak? The word is the most powerful tool you have as a human; it is a tool of magic."* — Don Miguel Ruiz, *The Four Agreements*

Listening vs. Hearing

We all know that sound is vibration. When you say a word: dance, hate, boy, love, it's infused with the pitch of the speaker's voice, their volume, even their attitude toward the word. Contrast for yourself the pitch, tone, and volume of Hitler's speeches vs. the warm, rolling tone of Morgan Freeman's voice. It isn't just their words, but the vibration they've created with their voices. These vibrations become words in your head in a magical way, exciting the tiny hair cells in your inner ear, which change the vibrations into electrical signals sent to the auditory center of your brain. You not only hear, "The dishes are still sitting in the sink." If you are listening, you might also hear, in the tone, pitch, and volume, "How come I always end up being the one who cleans up? You've left these dishes for a whole day; I'm sick and tired of it!" even though none of those words were spoken.

The ability to listen to others is indeed a superpower. But the ability to listen to yourself is the key to the kingdom. There are two parts to this power: listening to the words you hear or say, and listening to the words in your head.

> *"For one alert to its essential meaning, the properly chosen word has*
> *a magical effectiveness; but if the essential meaning is distorted,*
> *a (person's) whole behavior may be distorted in consequence."* —
> Isha Schwaller DeLubicz, *The Opening of the Way*

Isha Schwaller DeLubicz was an Egyptologist who lived in Luxor for about fifteen years, decoding the hieroglyphics and studying how the ancient Egyptians used language. The Egyptians believed that words were literally magic, with both the written symbol and the utterance having innate power. If the word itself carries a vibration, then we are constantly receiving and transmitting energy through our words.

"I think you should be putting the egg yolks in one at a time."

"That's not the way I do it."

"Whoa! Why are you angry with me?

You thought you spoke calmly, sensibly, "That's not the way I do it," but your friend sensed your resentment. Somewhere in the back of your head, as your friend spoke, you were experiencing an inner "chatter" that influenced the words that came out of your mouth. It's so fast, and so subtle, that often it's only later that you realize that you were feeling criticized, that you perceived your friend as being unfair, and that you felt defensive and wanted to lash out. They couldn't possibly know how your mother hovered over you telling you were doing it all wrong as you tried to learn something. Or that you were punished if you came home with a less than perfect report card. Your entire history (OK, my entire history) can be encapsulated in a conversation about egg yolks.

There are the words you speak and hear. And then there are the words in your head. How do you begin to listen to the words inside of you before you speak the words? In the background of your mind, there is a constant, persistent chatter that actually influences your relationship with yourself and the world. These are not the words you mutter as you are wandering down the cereal aisle, "Cocoa Puffs, Fruit Loops, good lord, don't they have any sugar-free cereal in here?" These are not even the words you say in a moment of self-discovery when no one is there, "OMG, I can't believe I missed the turn! I'm an idiot!"

What was going on in your head as you missed the turn? People say they were spacing out. But it is likely that words were dancing through your brain as you drove past. This constant rumination impacts our self-esteem, our pain levels, and our mood. These inner conversations form the background that creates the reality you see, impacting your mood, controlling your worldview.

Neuroscientist Antonio Damasio said, "A background feeling is not what we feel when we jump out of our skin for sheer joy, or when we are despondent over lost love; both of these actions correspond to emotional body states. A background feeling corresponds instead to the body state prevailing between emotions. When we feel happiness, anger, or another emotion, the background feeling has been superseded by an emotional feeling. The background feelings probably contribute to a mood, good, bad or indifferent."[xix] In other words, a foreground feeling is a clear reaction that you recognize. You win the lottery. Woo-hoo! You feel really, really happy. But big, recognizable foreground emotions are not always present. But there's a background feeling that lives in your mood, in your attitude, and you don't always see it. It's the same thing when you are speaking; your words seem to come from the foreground. But in the background, you have other words going on in your head, or you have other feelings that are related to the words that you're sharing. As mentioned in Chapter 3, Damasio's research also shows that we experience somatic reactions in our bodies even before we're aware of our feelings or thoughts: for example, how sweat appears before you are conscious of being nervous, or of how you gesture *before* you say the words.

Do You Hear What I Hear?

In previous chapters, we talked about the difference between sensation and perception in relation to pain. Perception applies to what you hear as well. How many times have you been involved in an argument when one of you said, "But that's not what I meant!" How many times have you been with friends, recounting a story, and someone said, "Wait, that's not what he said!" You can have perfect hearing, but if the words come in through your personal filter, you will interpret them with your own perceptions of what is taking place.

There are two kinds of listening. You can, in other words, be ready to jump in with an answer, a response to what is being said. Or you can listen to understand, allowing the words—or the silence in some cases—to sink in, to listen to how the words reverberate in you, to listen to the foreground and background experience of yourself as you experience the words. This can be in the presence of others or in listening to yourself.

Feeling Our Words

By now, everyone has done dozens of these silly word puzzles, where you pick three words that jump out at you, and that in some way tell you who you are, or whether you will find love, or be a success. Let's play this game a little differently. Circle the first three words you see. Try to resist looking for other words. Write the three words down before reading further.

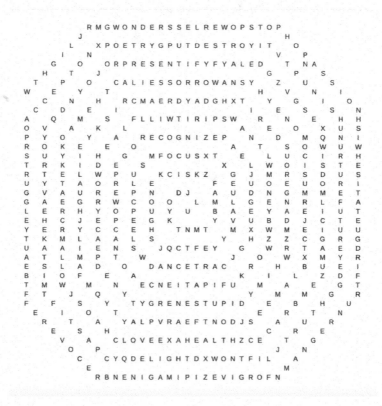

Look at your words. Do any of them have an emotional charge? Are you already ruminating or creating a story about those words? Are you trying to figure out what "this all means?" That process that you are feeling is called listening to respond. You are looking for the answer, even though you don't know the question yet.

Now that you have written your three words, say them out loud. Feel the vibration in yourself as you say each word. Where does it land in you? Maybe there *is* a story to that word for you. Maybe you feel dismissive, like this word has no meaning in your life right now.

Taking It In

- Stand up and begin to slowly turn to look around yourself. As you are turning, just take in the room. The room could be in the foreground of your attention. Or perhaps you have an ache or pain in your body as you turn, which then takes over the foreground. It may sound funny, but notice what you are noticing.

- Fold your arms across your chest.

- Does that change how you breathe? Crossing our arms affects listening in countless ways. A popular cliché is that if you cross your arms during a conversation it means your mind is closed. There can be truth to that. But folding or crossing the arms can be many things—depending on the foreground and background of your situation. You could be protecting yourself. We are the only animal that chooses to remain on two legs, exposing our vital organs to all comers. Even our closest cousins in the ape family can still drop to four legs to protect the front and run away. However, folding the arms can also be a soothing gesture, like hugging yourself. It can bring you back together to listen to yourself.

- In this self-hug position, hold onto the area your hand touches. It might be a piece of the ribcage. Or the top of your arm.

- Sense your breath again. You'll notice that this position inhibits the breathing in the front of your chest.

- Sense your back. Can you breathe so that the back ribs move out a little? Your lungs actually have more space in the back than the front. Often when we are trying to "listen" the front chest tightens, and the back, which is often not part of our brain map, stays frozen. Don't force, just imagine your lungs expanding as if they touch the ribs in the back and then move away.

- Begin to turn again, still holding on to yourself. You probably won't be able to turn as far as you did with your arms down. Sense the pulling in your ribs.

- Now make it smaller and faster, as if you were creating a sideways oscillation, right/left, light and quick.

- Pause and lower your arms.

- Notice your breath. Notice the movement in your chest. This is your foreground.

- For a moment, expand your attention and see if you can notice your emotions and thoughts that are in the background. Can you include the background in your foreground? Can you bring your emotions and thoughts into the foreground and maintain an awareness of your chest and breath in the background?

One way to bring awareness to your choices is to intentionally limit yourself. By closing your chest, you learn to breathe with other parts of yourself. By using your hands to constrain your rotation, you invite other parts to participate in the movement. Then when you let go, you can breathe better, move better, and therefore, listen better.

- Fold your arms the other way, switching the arm that is above the other. Try the same experiment.

- As you slowly turn, can you bring your three words into the foreground? Do you see them? Simply think them? Say them? As you speed up your rotation, what happens to the words? Paying attention, moving, and thinking at the same time can often feel challenging. Yet we are moving and thinking all the time without really acknowledging that one is in the background, influencing the other. By challenging yourself to expand your attention to include an awareness of both, you will be more able to listen to yourself and others.

When I work with individuals, listening is an essential part of the work. I listen of course to the story they tell, the sound of the words as they come out. At the same time, I'm listening to how they land in me. It is so easy to allow personal bias and filters to affect my ability to really hear someone. At the same time, I have to listen to something deeper. Sometimes their pain is below the pain they are telling me about.

Carla is an ER nurse with a passion for helping others. In her late 50s, "saving people's lives" is what she proudly says is her profession. Needless to say, when Covid hit, Carla's job became even more challenging. She came to see me because she had developed a strange pain under her right shoulder blade. The only way she was able to keep working and even sleep was to take muscle relaxants, which made her feel less alert. She, probably more than most people, was also well aware of the dangers of depending on pills. Of course, like so many people who come to a Feldenkrais teacher, Carla had already tried several other modalities with little to no relief.

As I listened to Carla talk about the demands of her job, I found myself breathing higher in my chest, as if I was living her ER story, which was somewhere between a screwball comedy and Nightmare on Elm Street. I unconsciously wrapped my arms around my chest and hunched a bit. A fleeting thought came in, "Are you protecting yourself from this?" But I could suddenly feel my back expanding as I took a deep breath. Yes, maybe I was tightening my "emotional armor" as I heard her story, but then I spontaneously used the hug to allow myself to recalibrate and open to more of Carla's story.

As we worked together that day, we explored movements connecting the chest to the shoulders and the breath. The chest, shoulders, and breath are key components of our emotional expression. Suddenly, I saw tears on her face. Worried that I had taken it too far, I asked if she needed tissues, space, or rest. Suddenly, another story poured out. About her abusive husband, for whom she was never good enough. About her son who was never in touch and was probably an alcoholic. About her sense of guilt and failure that she was "saving lives" every day, but her family was crumbling.

I held the space for her as she poured out her pain. Then instead of dialog, I invited her to move in various ways while embracing herself. When she sat up, the pain was gone. We have continued working together. The pain returns, but now she is equipped with strategies for relief as well as an awareness that she was "holding it together" in too many arenas. She is also working with a counselor to move through what will be a challenging shift in her family dynamics.

Taking Your Superpower Into the World

"What the world needs now, is love, sweet love

That's the only thing that there's just too little of . . ."

– Jackie DeShannon

If you Google empathic listening, you will find everything from "Nine easy steps to empathic listening" to "learn to show empathy for a successful talk." Even empathy can become a manipulative tactic. Showing empathy is not feeling empathy. Instead of trying to "be empathic" simply listen with attention—to the words, to the person speaking, to your inner thoughts.

Paul Ekman, a psychologist who specializes in body language, says there is no such emotion called love. Unlike emotions, which change minute to minute, he says that love is ". . . a commitment. Loving your children doesn't mean that you might be afraid of the risks that they take, annoyed when they don't show up for a meeting with you, sad when they are disappointed, and happy when they succeed."

Listening with attention can be an *act* of love. When you are attending to yourself: listening to your breathing, sensing your place in space, aware of your facial expressions and your gestures as you engage with your friend, partner, boss, child, you are altering the vibration of the interaction as well as your own inner chemistry. This is truly alchemy. When you are able to "listen" in this way, you and the object of your attention can be transformed.

> *"At this moment, there appears an energy coming from a higher emotional current, irresistible as long as it is obeyed. It is this energy, a cosmic force passing in us, that all traditions call 'love.'"* —Jeanne DeSalzmann

Isn't that what the world needs now?

CHAPTER 13

The Healer's Superpower – Vitality

"What drains your spirit, drains your body. What fuels your spirit, fuels your body." – Carolyn Myss

Take a look at your hands. Whether you spend all day connecting your fingers to keyboards or are building a house, the miracle of your hands and the power they contain is the key to humanity's power. There is evidence that language skills evolve with the ability to grasp.[xx] We even have it in our language: when you grasp a concept or grasp for truth. Your hands connect you to the world when you seize the moment or hold fast to your ideals.

By intentionally connecting with your hands, you can begin to access the healer's superpower of vitality. Your perception of your vitality influences your self-image. Scientists and doctors will quantify it with explanations of neurotransmitters, hormones, and brain and nervous system function. But you feel it as energy, anxiety, depression, and well-being. It is the quality of your life force.

Using Your Power

Your hands connect your vitality to others as well as feed it back to your own self. Remember a time when you saw someone you were absolutely delighted to see in the distance? You started waving your hand at them, maybe even jumping up and down, as if your waving and enthusiasm would bring them toward you even faster. You sent your vitality out toward the object of your desire through your hand.

Hold your hands in front of you and begin shaking them up and down, really flopping them. Do it in unison, then alternate, moving them so one hand is going down while the other hand is going up, as if you were throwing your hands around flopping from the wrists. Pause and feel your hands. Take your energized hands and begin patting yourself. Shoulders, chest, face, thighs—wherever you can reach. You can increase or decrease the force of the pat according to your comfort level. Pause and sense how everywhere you touched has a different quality.

By expressing your thoughts and emotions, your hands are sharing the life force that starts with those hormones and neurotransmitters that create your self-image. Even if you think you don't use your hands much, they are busy sharing your thoughts with the world.

I was once teaching a body language workshop. There was a young man in the class who was particularly animated. He would share his discoveries while wildly gesticulating. We were in a group discussion about the functions of the hands and the power of gesture. He shrugged and said, "I dunno. I don't really use my hands much when I talk." The entire class burst into spontaneous laughter. He threw his hands up, saying, "What? It's true!" Then he looked at his hands up in the air. "Do I use my hands that much?" he asked. The class applauded . . . with their hands of course.

Often our unconscious gestures reveal that our emotions are different than our words. Pundits often have a field day analyzing the disconnect between a politician's words and gestures. The gestures of the hand that connect with your thoughts and emotions are a manifestation of what's taking place inside you. When you reach out to someone, how do you reach: if it's your lover who just proposed marriage? Or announced they want to break up? Your child about to fall? Your friend right after they told you a ridiculous story? Your hands are powerful, and they can be the conduit for healing yourself and others.

Put Your Hands Together

In Chapter 4, when you explored bringing your hands together and apart, sensing the buildup of energy, *chi*, life force between them. We bring our hands together to applaud, in reaction to news, in eager anticipation, in prayer. The hands coming together in prayer can be an invocation or a greeting. When you touch your palms together, you are connecting the right and left hemispheres of your brain. You could say you are bringing your thoughts together, creating a neural circuit. When you worry, you wring your hands, as if you're trying to wring the thoughts out and find a solution.

When you've conquered or won, you clasp your hands and raise them up in victory, literally connecting and elevating your thoughts and feelings. "Sit at your desk with your hands folded, young lady," suddenly takes on new meaning. Is it possible that our grammar school teachers intuited that folding your hands would help calm your thoughts? We rub our hands together in anticipation or in preparation for a big task. A social custom that seems to be disappearing is the handshake. Covid has perhaps been the final straw on an ancient custom that is going the way of the bow, tipping the hat, and kissing the hand. It used to be standard practice to reach out and shake someone's hand upon meeting them. People even evaluated a person's vitality by the quality of the clasp, by the firmness of the grip. Now we stand and give a little nod, or an awkward wave, or bump elbows.

Going Deeper

How do you use your hands for communication to others or yourself?

Have your hands ever betrayed your thoughts?

How many times a day do you bring your hands together?

While different cultures employ various gestures as representations of ideas or language (flipping the bird, the fig, etc.) these gestures are a substitute for words, like sign language. One gesture that crosses cultures and exemplifies the power of your hands for communication and healing is putting your hands together in prayer. When you put your hands together in prayer and bow to someone saying "namaste," it means "I salute the divine in you." You direct your fingers, the power of your mind, to that person. When your fingers point upward, you are invoking a higher force.

Bringing your hands together helps you access the superpower of vitality. You are connecting your parts with intention. The energy that flows from your hands moves from your pelvis through your chest (your power and emotions) to send the current that moves out of your hands. When you invoke through prayer, you organize your mind to make your action congruent with your intention.

> *"The most powerful prayer, one well-nigh omnipotent and the worthiest work of all, is the outcome of a quiet mind. The quieter it is the more powerful, the worthier, the deeper, the more telling and more perfect the prayer is. To the quiet mind all things are possible."*

Meister Eckhart

Empowering Your Hands

- Bring your hands together in the prayer position.

- Slowly raise your arms toward the ceiling and then lower them in front of you. You don't have to lift high, just enough to feel the upward motion. Where do your eyes want to go? What do you feel in other parts of yourself?

- Let your hands rest on your lap. Lower your head and allow your back to round. Roll your pelvis back as you allow your belly to sink back toward your spine, softly, on an exhale, then return to sitting upright. Notice the sensation of sinking into yourself.

- Now try the opposite. Push your stomach out, arch your back, and look up at the ceiling without straining your neck.

- Go back and forth between these two ways of using your torso, rising and sinking.

- Rest.

- Put your hands together in prayer again, and raise your arms. This time, keep your eyes on your hands, letting your head look up to the ceiling as your hands elevate. Allow your back to arch a bit as you did a moment ago. What do you feel in your chest? Is this a familiar gesture for you or novel?

- As you lower your hands down, lower your head, continuing to keep your eyes connected to your hands. Does your back change its shape?

- If you haven't already, begin to include arching and rounding your spine.

- Repeat it a few times, noticing your breath and allowing yourself to pause in the various postures.

- Rest for a while.

- Bring your hands back into the prayer position. This time as you raise your hands, bow your head and round your back. Your hands may not go as high.

- As you lower your hands toward your chest, look up. How is this experience of "prayer" different?

- Place your palms on the area of your *dantian* (an inch or so below the belly button) and move them away a few times, sensing your hands' connection with your power center. Let your hands hover in front of the *dantian* and repeat the rounding of your back

- As your pelvis rolls back, bring your hands toward your belly as if you were bringing something into your belly.

- Push your belly forward and arch your back, opening your hands and extending them as if you were offering something.

- You are receiving and then giving. Absorbing and emanating. You can make it very small.

- Notice how you use your hands. You could be protecting, supporting, giving, or receiving. You can make this movement tiny and almost invisible, allowing the connection of your hands to the primal part of you.

- Pause.

- Bring your hands to your solar plexus, the spot just under your ribs. Repeat the same movement of rounding your back.

- Allow the hands to move, to bring something in.

- As you arch your back, open your hands and reach a little forward.

- Notice your breath. Again, it can be a very small movement. What do you take in into your solar plexus, the center of your will, of your ego, of your personality? You can harness the ego to help heal, support, bless, and forgive.

- You can include a movement of your head or leave it vertical.

- Rest.

- Bring your hands to your heart. Just pause there a moment. Just pause and feel. When you connect the hands to the heart, you connect three pulses; your heart, your lungs, and the pulse in your wrists are all entraining together.

- Let your hands push your chest slightly backward as you bow your head. Wait there. Are you forgiving or asking to be forgiven?

- Then open the chest, opening the hands, allowing them to come a little forward.

- Repeat it a few times, sensing the breath, softening the chest, allowing the stomach to relax, the belly to go down.

- Reverse.

- Pause.

- Picture an energy or power moving up from the sacral area, up through the solar plexus, out the heart.

- Bring your hands to prayer. As you round, bow.

- Expand your chest, arch your back slightly, and let your hands open out into whatever blessing feels appropriate.

- Bring your hands to your face without quite touching it. Sense the space between your face and your hands, moving your hands gently toward and away. Can you picture how your face is composed? Does it feel closed or open?

- Move your hands away and look up, allowing the hands to move up and out.

- Bring everything back in. If it feels right, allow this movement to grow a bit bigger, and imagine that your face can also expand outward, as if the hands themselves are calling the muscles of your face to expand, and then as your hands return, "recompose" your face.

- Notice your breath. When you trust your breath, connect to your torso, and sense your hands, you can experience vitality moving through you. You become beauty, elegance, grace, like a blessing.

Taking Your Superpower into the World

It sometimes seems like there is no end to the suffering in the world, from gigantic catastrophes and violence to the intimate tragedies in our personal lives. While there have been individuals throughout history, from Jesus to Edgar Cayce, who have manifested a level of vitality for healing body and soul, they could not save the entire world. But you can use your vitality to be a shining beacon for those around you. Each time you extend your hand to someone with the intention of connecting, each time you offer a helping hand allowing the movement to emanate from your heart and through yourself to the other person, you are using your superpower. When you take your lover's hands in yours, or caress your child's face, or bathe your dying parent, sensing how your vitality moves up through you and out to them, you are a healer. Namaste.

CHAPTER 14

The Visionary's Superpower: Perspective

"If the path before you is clear, you're probably on someone else's." – Joseph Campbell

Vasari was one of the first art historians in the early Renaissance. He wrote about the sacking of Rome, "As if these disasters were not enough, Rome then suffered the anger of Totila." We've all heard of Attila, but who ever heard of Totila? I thought it was a typo, but there actually was a general named Totila, who didn't seem to make it into my grammar school history book. "The walls of the city were destroyed. Its finest and most noble buildings were razed to the ground with fire and sword. And then it was burnt from one end to the other, left bereft of every living creature and abandoned to the ravages of their conflagration. For the space of 18 days, not a living thing moved. Totila tore down and destroyed the city's marvelous statues, its pictures, mosaics and stuccos. As a result, Rome lost I will not say its majesty, but rather its identity and its very life."

Between Christianity's efforts to eliminate the legacy of paganism, and the ravages of conquering tribes from the east, ancient knowledge was virtually destroyed, so that the people from around 400 until around 1200 CE literally lost perspective. They had no record of what had happened in the past. Therefore, they also had no sense of the future. It really was like living in Groundhog Day for a couple of hundred years. These were the Dark Ages.

This lack of perspective is reflected in the art of that time.

You can see in the illustration that it is actually a story of two different battles at two different times and locations. But the artists mixed it all together, because to them, time and space were all the same thing.

Living in "the present moment" has to include perspective, a knowing that the present moment has a history and a future. It is an interesting coincidence (if there is such a thing) that when artists discovered perspective, science and math began to recover some of the ancient wisdom that had been lost to those Dark Ages.

Seeing and Thinking

To have perspective means to be able to actually see in depth: behind yourself, in front of yourself, around yourself. You are able to see the big picture and details; you can literally see the forest *and* the trees.

The eyes are the center of presence for the visionary, literally and metaphorically. The movement of your eyes is connected to your spine, brain, and nervous system. Even though you're using our eyes all the time, you don't necessarily sense how your eyes are affecting your perspective. Your eyes are moving all the time, tracking outer and inner information, connecting to your thought processes. They reveal your perspective on situations.

Practitioners of NLP, neurolinguistic programming, track the movement of the eyes and our inner stories, So do lawyers in the courtroom! Each movement of your eyes sends messages to your nervous system about your perspective on what you see, even though you are rarely conscious of it.

For example, there are a thousand ways to say "I don't know." As you explore each of the following, pause a moment and allow your posture to connect with your eyes before you say, "I don't know."

- Move your eyes to the right as you say, "I don't know."

- Look down and repeat, "I don't know."

- Look up as you say it and sense if it feels different than when you look down.

- Turn your head to one side and move your eyes the other way and say, "I don't know."

- Lower your head, lift your eyes and say, "I don't know."

- Play with other positions if you want to. Each time, your eyes change the meaning! Your eyes are trying to get a perspective on an answer as you say, "I don't know."

- This is just one example of what is taking place all the time.

Going Deeper

Is there something in your life right now that needs a new perspective?

It could be about your personal history. It could be a current situation. It could be something you're planning for the future. Don't think too hard.

Whatever pops up in your head is the most important one. As you contemplate this question, close your eyes. Sense your eyes resting in your skull. Use your inner vision to view this challenge, this possibility, this question. Notice as you're thinking how your eyes work with your thought process, how they want to jump around as different aspects of the question or the problem appear. The eyes move with the thoughts. Take a few minutes and write down your situation, and how you are thinking and feeling about it.

Developing Perspective

Your left and right brain process information differently, and scientists suggest that how you create your perception of the world begins with your eyes. The left brain latches onto individual things, then identifies and names them: lamp, car, tiger. The right brain takes in the whole picture. Of course we want them working together. To be able to clearly see both details and the big picture widens your perspective, allowing you to process information about your worlds, both inner and outer, more effectively. This sequence is best experienced with your eyes closed, so take the opportunity to click on the qr code and just follow along.

- Sit in a comfortable position. If you're on the floor, you may want to lean against a wall and prop your elbows on your knees. If you are sitting in an armchair, you can prop your elbows on the arms of the chair. Otherwise, just bend your elbows so that your forearms are bent, your hands somewhere out in front, your palms relaxed.

- Imagine you are holding a string with your right hand, and this string somehow extends up to your face and connects with your right eye. It's easier to do this with eyes closed, so read each direction, then try it with your eyes closed.

- Imagine that on the string is a bead or a pearl. In your mind's eye, move that pearl down to your fingers, then slowly move it toward your eye.

- With your eyes closed, reach with your left hand and grab the bead, then open your eyes and see where you grabbed.

- Holding the bead, begin to slide your hand up and down. You can do this with eyes open or closed. Or try both.

- Rest.

- Repeat this with a string in the left hand.

- Rest.

- Can you watch the beads on both strings simultaneously?

- Rest.

- What happens when you cross the strings and take the string for your right eye into your left hand and the string for your left eye into your right hand? Where do the beads cross?

If you're feeling cross-eyed by now, you are not alone. But often this kind of exercise improves your ability to see in three dimensions. People with stereoblindness don't have the same perspective. As you bring the right and left eye and right and left brain together, you can begin to open your perspective to seeing your own life with greater clarity.

- Take another moment to look around your room. How do your eyes feel? How does the room look?

- You may want to return to what you wrote earlier and see if you have a different perspective on your situation or story now.

Taking Your Superpower into the World

We currently live in a polarized society. We use the terms "right" and "left" to signify attitudes, belief systems, and points of view. It is interesting that the left brain governs the right eye, which in animals is always looking for danger or prey. When birds sense a predator, they turn their right eye toward the threat to assess it.[xxi] The right eye sees the world as a potential threat or conquest. The left eye is looking more broadly, at possibility and options. In an ideal world, the two eyes work together; otherwise, perspective is lacking.

Can you remain centered and really see another person's perspective? Can you offer a clear perspective on a situation? You can use your eyes as your personal feedback when you find yourself in a situation that needs a new perspective. Have they narrowed? Are they rolling in contempt? Are they looking toward the exit? Are they frozen like a deer in headlights? Soften your gaze. Look left and right before you speak. Can you literally "see" their point of view? It's possible to transform a situation without doing anything more than seeing the whole picture.

PART IV

Your Map,
Your Territory

Your brain is constantly mapping and remapping your self-image.[xxii] How you are is how you see your world. This neuroplasticity means that you are creating your experience as you are perceiving it. Abracadabra. The four archetypes are a portal into your possibility, your allies, and sometimes your obstacles, on your journey through this uncharted landscape of yourself. This journey will go more smoothly if you leave your baggage behind. Just take an empty bag to gather the gifts you will receive along the way.

Russian folk tales contain many versions of the story of Ivan the Fool. The youngest of three brothers, he is depicted as simple and naïve. The brothers, of course, are crafty and greedy. Trouble comes to the kingdom in many variations, depending on the tale: the theft of the golden apples, the abduction of the sister, or the attack of the firebird. The king promises half the kingdom to whoever accomplishes the deed of setting things right. The two brothers, in turn, set out on the journey and fail because they think they know better, or because in a crucial moment, they fall asleep, or their greed leads them to fail. Ivan, being simple, but not foolish, is the one who listens to the old woman, talks to the stone, chooses the wolf and, of course, wins the princess and the kingdom. (Although sometimes, his greedy brothers try to steal his legacy, adding more spice to the story.) By being open, he succeeds in his hero's journey.

As you navigate your own journey, you will discover that your map *is* your territory. Your obstacles and your allies are within you. Everything you need is literally at your fingertips. Bon Voyage!

CHAPTER 15

The Journey is the Destination

It may not feel like it, but the trajectory of your life is a giant odyssey of metaphors, symbols, and teachings. Just because you haven't climbed Mt. Everest, slain dragons, or gone on a mythic quest for the Holy Grail, the adventure of your own story is not diminished. At every stage of your life, there are desires, dreams, and choice points that influence your life trajectory. In Chapter 6 you faced your shadow in the exercise of recapitulation, going backward over your day to see those hidden moments of self-sabotage. Now is the opportunity to look ahead.

The four archetypes live inside the human experience and can be either a touchstone or an obstacle to your journey. Where are you now? Where do you wish to be? Who do you wish to be? The map below is a simple illustration of your path.

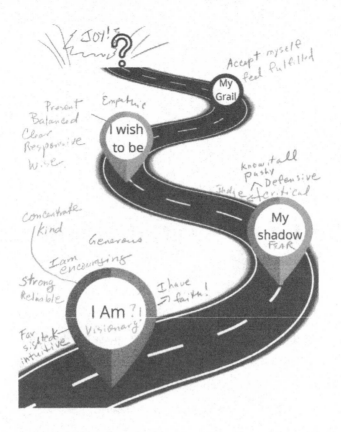

We all know that that there are wrong turns, detours, dead ends and more that can appear. You can either print this map by scanning it here, draw

your own map, or simply use this illustration as a reference as you go through the following questions and explore in your journal. The process below can be revisited each time you find you have lost your way or feel ready to embark on a new journey.

I AM

These two words are a powerful *mantra* in many ancient traditions. The Hebrew God Yahweh was called "I am Who am." "I am" is a reminder that

I exist. It sounds silly, but if you don't remember that you exist, you are like a placeholder character in a video game. I AM.

It is also a statement of who and what you are. In this moment. Can you list some truths about yourself right now?

For example:

I AM: generous, considerate, kind, strong, reliable, intuitive, stubborn, fearful, wounded, ashamed.

These are my words. What are yours?

Close your eyes. Inwardly say, "I AM." As the words to complete your sentence appear, jot them down. You can write on the illustration or in your journal.

As you look at your words, ask yourself which archetypes come to mind. Are they superpowers or kryptonite?

Generous, kind, considerate – Teacher

Strong, reliable, stubborn, fearful – Warrior

Intuitive – Visionary

Wounded, ashamed – Healer

We carry the four archetypes on our life journey. We just have to remember they are there.

Sit in meditation for a moment and feel the power of I AM.

My Shadow

Sometimes your shadow is connected to the kryptonites you identified above. Sometimes it really can be your alternate view of reality. You have to remember that your shadow has no dimension; it's the darkness you use to hide your true light. It keeps you from moving forward toward your personal grail. As you look at the qualities you listed above, is there one particular kryptonite that pierces you, that feels especially uncomfortable?

For example, mine is fear. People often tell me how amazed they are at the risks I take in my career, in my writing. They call me fearless. But I know that underneath, I carry the terror of my past, which manifests in my shadow. When I am possessed by my shadow, I engage in behavior from my dark side. My Shadow behaviors:

Being a "know it all" - Teacher

Acting pushy - Warrior

Being critical or judgmental - Teacher

Being competitive - Warrior

Being defensiveness – Warrior/Healer

As I look at my shadow behaviors, I can see that my fear is a combination of the warrior and teacher kryptonites. Take a moment to self-reflect and make your own list.

As you look at your list, what jumps out at you? Are you willing to literally "see your shadow?" If you recognize an archetype, go back to their related chapters and explore the exercises again. Or just take a moment to embrace your shadow self.

Me and My Shadow

Your shadow has been working hard to protect you, even though as you look at its qualities, you may not want to believe that its intentions are good. It can be hard to let go of, and you certainly can't force this. An interesting way to dance with your shadow is to acknowledge it. Denying your shadow will only make it more defiant.

Take a piece of paper, or your journal, and begin a letter to your shadow. You can start with Dear Shadow, or maybe you even have a name for it. (I actually sometimes call my Shadow Lidia, which was my mother's name, since she was so often my role model for shadow behavior!) You can thank it for its years of protecting you. And then you can explain why you'd like it to get a little smaller, maybe even take a break. Of course, you are really speaking to a part of your brain.

Don't worry about trying to "change yourself." The process of seeing and acknowledging is the beginning of your transformation.

I Wish to Be

Perhaps you remember the story of Pinocchio, the marionette whose greatest wish was to be "a real boy." While his wish was real, he sabotaged himself left and right on his journey, lured by promises of selfish pleasures that always went wrong. It took overcoming his shadow to transform. Certain esoteric traditions suggest that this ancient mantra is literally a reminder that we are caught in a world of illusion, and we also have to remember to wish to be a real human being. "I wish to be" is like calling possibility to yourself, whether you simply say those words or add a further intention.

What/who do you wish to be? This can take many forms:

I wish to be:

A better writer

A lawyer

A world traveler

Or it can be a state:

I wish to be:

In love

Pain free

Joyful

Or you could look at the previous parts of your journey, and evoke for yourself qualities you would like to integrate:

I wish to be:

Compassionate

Empathic

Balanced

Responsive

By declaring your wish, you are taking a step toward manifestation.

Your Grail

Your personal grail is your deepest dream. Sometimes dreams are so deeply buried, they've been forgotten. They got pushed aside, given up on early in life. Maybe it was circumstance, perhaps it was experiencing personal limitations that turned you away from your dream. That doesn't mean that now, as you contemplate your grail, you have to revisit your childhood fantasies of becoming a fireman or a ballerina. But perhaps that feeling of being of service, of bravery and strength, or grace and agility, can be accessed to fulfill a dream for today. You might not feel a need for outer accomplishment. It may be a desire to feel satisfied with who you are right now or to overcome a fear or speak a truth you have kept hidden all your life. As I studied this map, I recognized that in spite of all the things I've done, a belief that I am "not good enough" lay buried underneath. Freeing myself of this belief has become my grail. What is yours?

????

As you move into the unknown what lies ahead for you, what emotional state or feeling would feel good for you? Resilience? Joy? Power? See yourself moving through your life. Find one word and embrace it. That will be the beginning of your next quest!

CHAPTER 16

You Are A Star

"The nitrogen in our DNA, the calcium in our teeth, the iron in our blood, the carbon in our apple pies were made in the interiors of collapsing stars. We are made of star stuff." – Carl Sagan

As far back as Pythagoras, the pentagram, or five-pointed star has been as a representation for the human being. The top point is the head, and the other four points are the limbs, with the center being the trunk.

The four archetypes' centers of presence live in this symbol.

- Your pelvis and lower extremities – The Warrior

- Your chest and back – The Teacher

- Your hands – The Healer

- Your eyes – The Visionary

But nothing operates independently. Like a star, everything is in perpetual motion, and all the archetypes are constantly interacting with each other. This dynamic movement and relationship provides endless possibilities for deepening your practice.

The visionary needs the courage of the warrior, the wisdom of the teacher, and the energy of the healer to realize their vision. The healer needs the compassion of the teacher, the strength of the warrior, and the clarity of the visionary to let go of wounds. This ceaseless communication among centers follows the nervous system information highway.

Connecting your Centers of Presence

Different traditions speak of different collections of centers: Thinking, feeling, and sensing; the seven *chakras*; the *dantians*. Developing your awareness of your archetypal centers can inform and enrich your practice. When you begin to explore the power of relating your centers to each other, you can move through life with power, wisdom, vitality, and insight, no matter the challenge.

- Lie down to allow your anti-gravity muscles to let go. Take a moment, with eyes closed to sense yourself. Notice your weight, shape, breath, and breadth. Sense your face and allow the muscles of your face to also yield to gravity, so that both sides of your face move out and down. Remember your original face.

- Recall the exercise from Chapter 1 where you drew five lines emanating from your belly: down each leg, up the center of yourself, and down your arms.

- Allow your arms to move out a bit from your body to assume your star shape. Bring your attention to your warrior center, sensing your pelvic region. Notice where your attention goes: to the bones as they rest on the floor, the abdominal area, the pelvic floor, the belly button, the movement of the breath. Feel the life force there.

- Then move that life force and your attention upward to your chest, your teacher center. Allow your presence to fill the rib cage and sense your lungs, the beating of your heart, and the movement of your diaphragm and how it massages your organs. Notice the feelings that come up when you give your center this loving attention.

- From your chest, let that sensation flow up through your arms and out to your hands. Sense the center of each palm, as if a golden fire nestled there then moves through your fingers.

- Bring your arms up to the ceiling and join your palms, and as the hands connect, move that power into your head, sending it up the center of your skull to your forehead where like a fountain, it flows up and cascades down, encircling your eyes. Bring your arms down. For a moment rest in this flow.

- Then picture the many times in your life you've drawn a five-pointed star. Maybe you haven't done it since childhood. Following one line to create the image. Imagine that line as a current now and follow it, starting at any point: your right hand, your left leg—it doesn't matter. Let your line of energy move as if you were illuminating your entire being, passing through each of your centers of presence. You are a star.

And Finally

As you have developed awareness of your centers of presence, your access to your inner resources and possibilities have increased. The embodiment practices that you have learned can be repeated as often as you need in order to access an archetype's energy. As you inhabit each center of presence, acknowledge your kryptonites, and embrace your superpowers, you will own one of the most powerful tools existence has to offer: choice. This is what leads to

transformation. Stand in your power, breathe with compassion, reach out and touch others as you apply your brilliant perspective. You have the power, wisdom, vitality, and insight to choose to be the change you want to see in the world.

Acknowledgments

When I was a little girl, my Father's nickname for me was "Sama." It's the Polish word for alone. Apparently, even as an infant, I would push away anyone's offer to help, saying "Sama, sama." Learning to listen to and to trust others has been part of my own personal growth arc. There are two writers' groups who have nurtured my writing for years and these wonderful women have read so many iterations of my manuscript they deserve to be canonized. And my dear husband Ron Morecraft once again provided beautiful illustrations to accompany the lessons. Thank you, all!

End Notes

i   Acta Paediatrica, 2013, Language experienced in utero affects vowel perception after birth: a two-country study, Christine Moon, Hugo Lagercrantz, Patricia K Kuhl pp. 156–160. (http://ilabs.uw.edu/sites/default/files/2012%20Moon%20et%20al.pdf).

ii   "Mandibular and Maxillary Growth after Changed Mode of Breathing," *American Journal of Orthodontics and Dentofacial Orthopedics* 100, no. 1 (July 1991): 1–18; Shapiro, "Effects of Nasal Obstruction on Facial Development," 967–68.

iii   Siccardi MA, Tariq MA, Valle C., "Anatomy, Bony Pelvis and Lower Limb, Psoas Major." In: *StatPearls*. StatPearls Publishing, Treasure Island (FL); 2021. PMID: 30571039.

iv   Snijders, T., Aussieker, T., Holwerda, A., Parise, G., van Loon, L., & Verdijk, L. B. (2020). "The concept of skeletal muscle memory: Evidence from animal and human studies." *Acta physiologica (Oxford, England), 229* (3), e13465. https://doi.org/10.1111/apha.13465.

v   https://www.sciencedirect.com/topics/neuroscience/esophageal-plexus.

vi   Linkenhoker, Brie & Knudsen, Eric. (2002). "Incremental training increases the plasticity of the auditory space map in adult barn owls." *Nature. 419.* 293–6. 10.1038/nature01002.

vii   Julian F. Thayer, Fredrik Åhs, Mats Fredrikson, John J. Sollers, Tor

D. Wager, "A meta-analysis of heart rate variability and neuroim-aging studies: Implications for heart rate variability as a marker of stress and health," *Neuroscience & Biobehavioral Reviews, Volume 36, Issue 2,2012,*Pages 747–756, ISSN 0149–7634.

viii Alshami AM. "Pain: Is It All in the Brain or the Heart?" Curr Pain Headache Rep. 2019 Nov 14;23 (12):88. doi: 10.1007/s11916-019-0827-4. PMID: 31728781.

ix Laura Bond, *The Emotional Body*, 2017.

x Damasio AR. "The somatic marker hypothesis and the possible functions of the prefrontal cortex." *Philos Trans R Soc Lond B Biol Sci. 1996,* Oct 29;351(1346):1413-20. doi: 10.1098/rstb.1996.0125. PMID: 8941953.

xi Iain McGilchrist, The Master and His Emissary, pg. 189.

xii Ibid.

xiii Aulinas A. Physiology of the Pineal Gland and Melatonin. [Updated 2019 Dec 10]. In: Feingold KR, Anawalt B, Boyce A, et al., editors. Endotext [Internet]. South Dartmouth (MA): MDText.com, Inc.; 2000–. Available from: https://www.ncbi.nlm.nih.gov/books/NBK550972/.

xiv Kanai, R., Feilden, T., Firth, C., & Rees, G. (2011). Political orientations are correlated with brain structure in young adults. *Current biology: CB, 21*(8), 677–680. https://doi.org/10.1016/j.cub.2011.03.017.

xv Iain McGilchrist, The Master and His Emissary, pp 77–83.

xvi Dr. Robert Sapolsky: Science of Stress, Testosterone & Free Will | Huberman Lab Podcast #35 - https://www.youtube.com/watch?v=DtmwtjOoSYU.

xvii (Communicating in Business Today. R.G. Newman, MA Danzinger, M. Cohen (eds) DC Heath & Company, 1987).

xviii Mehrabian, Albert; Wiener, Morton (1967). "Decoding of Inconsistent Communications." *Journal of Personality and Social Psychology*. 6 (1): 109–114.

xix Damasio, Antonio, Descartes's Error, (1994), pg. 150–155.

xx Claudia L.R. Gonzalez, Melvyn A. Goodale, Hand preference for precision grasping predicts language lateralization, Neuropsychologia, Volume 47, Issue 14, 2009, Pages 3182 –3189.

xxi Tim Birkhead, "What Makes Bird Vision So Cool," *Audobon Magazine*, May–June 2013.

xxii Daniel J. Siegel, MD, Mindsight, 2011, pg. 244–248.

About the Author

 Lavinia's lifelong passion for understanding human expression, and how we can develop emotional resilience and maturity, began while growing up as the daughter of traumatized Holocaust survivors attempting to navigate the American dream. From a career in theater, her research took her towards the new field of somatic movement. She has taught the Feldenkrais Method® internationally for over 30 years, besides studying dozens of movement technologies from the healing, martial and performing arts. Immersing herself deeply in the work of somatic psychology, the power of mythology and the neuroscience of emotional expression, Lavinia has developed a somatic learning process called Kinēsa® which synthesizes her mind/body/emotion/spirit approach to deep personal healing and practical applications to life challenges. She lives in Asheville, NC with her husband, two cats and a flourishing garden of weeds.